Scriptures that Sing

by **Warren W. Wiersbe**
General Director
Back to the Bible

Back to the Bible

Lincoln, Nebraska 68501

65,000 printed to date—1986
(5-4325—65M—26)
ISBN 0-8474-6513-6

Cover design by Penguin Graphics
Cover photo by Reflections by Theo

Printed in the United States of America

Contents

Chapter 1

Why Christians Sing

The Christian faith is a singing faith. In fact, from the beginning to the end of the Bible, you will find songs of praise to God for who He is and for what He has done.

For example, when Israel was delivered from the land of Egypt, they met on the other side of the Red Sea and sang a hymn of praise to the Lord (see Ex. 15:1-21). The Book of Psalms is actually a collection of songs written by David and others. These psalms became the Jewish hymnbook for their worship services. Throughout the Old Testament we find the people praising God for their redemption and deliverance.

The New Testament also contains a number of hymns of adoration. We enjoy reading the beautiful song of Mary (see Luke 1:46-55), the praise of Zacharias (see vv. 68-79) and the exultation of the angels at the birth of the Lord Jesus (see 2:13,14). In addition, we find many references indicating the importance of music in the worship of the early church.

This pattern of praise has continued throughout church history. Many of the reformers realized the vast potential of music in Christian worship and in

5

the proclamation of the Gospel. One of the greatest reforms of Martin Luther was the restoration of congregational singing in evangelical churches. Today, Christians are still singing "A Mighty Fortress Is Our God" and many other hymns written by Luther. In addition to the revival they began in England, John and Charles Wesley are probably best known for their many marvelous hymns and Gospel songs. The effectiveness of the evangelistic crusades of D. L. Moody was due in part to the powerful singing of Ira Sankey. The Christian faith is indeed a singing faith.

A missionary friend of mine spent 25 years working among the African people of the Congo (now Zaire). When he first traveled up the river to the station where he was going to serve, he was met by the sounds of wailing, moaning, drumbeats and dismal songs. When my friend left the mission field to return home nearly a quarter of a century later, the people on both sides of the river were singing, "All hail the pow'r of Jesus' name, / Let angels prostrate fall; / Bring forth the royal diadem, / And crown Him Lord of all."

Because of Salvation

What motivates Christians to sing? According to the Scriptures, believers have four reasons for having a song in their hearts and praise on their lips. The first reason for singing is *because of salvation.* The psalmist knew the joy of salvation, for he wrote: "I waited patiently for the Lord; and he inclined unto me, and heard my cry. He brought me up also out of

6

an horrible pit, out of the miry clay, and set my feet upon a rock, and established my goings. And he hath put a new song in my mouth, even praise unto our God: many shall see it, and fear, and shall trust in the Lord" (Ps. 40:1-3).

This passage paints a perfect picture of the lost soul. Many unsaved people feel secure in their lives, not realizing that they are living in that horrible pit called "sin." They keep on sinking deeper and deeper in the miry clay until, one day, they will be swallowed up in judgment. But the Lord is standing by the pit, waiting to lift up anyone who will cry out to Him for help. When a person trusts in Christ, the Lord picks him up and sets him on the solid rock— Jesus Christ. He places his feet firmly on the path of life and guides his steps. Instead of a cry of desperation, the believer now has a song of praise to the Lord for His great salvation.

Throughout the Scriptures you will find that salvation is always accompanied by happiness. In Luke 15 Jesus told three parables that illustrated the joy people experience when the lost is found. When the shepherd found the one lost sheep, he rejoiced and even invited his neighbors in to celebrate with him (see vv. 3-6). Likewise, when the woman recovered the lost coin, she and her neighbors rejoiced (see vv. 8,9). When the Prodigal Son repented and returned home, his arrival was greeted with joyful singing and feasting (see vv. 11-24). In the same way, Jesus added, the angels in heaven rejoice when one sinner repents and comes to the Lord (see vv. 7,10).

Every person who has received Christ's salvation has a wonderful reason to sing. He is no longer living in the monotony of iniquity. The Lord has lifted him up from the bottom of that awful pit and has placed him on a safe and secure rock. The path that lays before him is full of promise because of God's grace. If you have experienced salvation and yet don't have a song in your heart, then something is wrong in your life. When you know Jesus as your Saviour, He gives you a song.

Because of the Scriptures

When a person is saved, the joy of knowing the Lord fills his heart with a song of thanksgiving. In addition, the Christian has a second reason for singing—*because of the Scriptures.* Colossians 3:15-17 says, "And let the peace of God rule in your hearts, to the which also ye are called in one body; and be ye thankful. Let the word of Christ dwell in you richly in all wisdom; teaching and admonishing one another in psalms and hymns and spiritual songs, singing with grace in your hearts to the Lord. And whatsoever ye do in word or deed, do all in the name of the Lord Jesus, giving thanks to God and the Father by him."

In this passage Paul taught that when the Word of God is dwelling in you, you will have a song. Through the Word of God we discover the God of the Word. And the more we learn of God's goodness and grace toward us, the more we will desire to sing praises to His name.

Not only are hymns useful in expressing our

8

thankfulness to God, but they are also a means of instruction and admonition. More people today get their theology from songs than they do from sermons. One of the reasons we are doing this study of famous hymns is to enable us to better understand the scriptural basis for these songs. Many of the hymn writers have taken passages from the Bible and have set them to music. This "musical Word" has been used by God to touch hearts and change lives in ways that the spoken Word could not do.

However, sometimes I fear that many people are receiving bad theology rather than sound instruction from some Christian music. Many so-called Christian songs today are not based on Scripture. Instead of teaching biblical truth, they are deceiving people with their false "gospel." A singer has no more right to sing a lie than a preacher has to preach a lie. No matter how beautiful a song may be, if it is not teaching biblical truth, then it has no place in our worship service.

When we have the peace of God (through salvation) and the Word of Christ (the Scriptures) in our heart, then we will sing from our heart to the Lord. As we sing, the Lord adds grace to our heart (see v. 16). Sometimes it takes grace to sing, especially when we are experiencing difficulty and suffering. No doubt it took grace for Paul and Silas to sing when they were in the Philippian prison (see Acts 16:22-25). Even the Lord Jesus Christ, when He was facing His darkest hour, was able to sing. Matthew 26:30 states, "And when they had sung an hymn, they went out into the mount of Olives." Can you imagine singing before going to a cross? Because the Lord possesses this kind of grace and because He freely gives it to His children, we are able to sing *in spite of* our suffering.

Because of the Holy Spirit

We sing because of salvation. If you are saved, you ought to have a song. We sing because of the Scriptures. If you are living in the Word of God and allowing the Word of God to live in you, then you should have a song. The third reason why we can sing is *because of the Holy Spirit*. In Ephesians 5:18,19 we find a passage that is parallel to the one in Colossians 3:15-17. It states, "And be not drunk with wine, wherein is excess; but be filled with the Spirit; speaking to yourselves in psalms and hymns and spiritual songs, singing and making melody in your heart to the Lord." These two passages are parallel because the Word of God is what the Spirit of God uses to generate life, power and victory in our hearts. When we are filled with the Spirit, then we will be controlled by the Word of God.

Those who are filled with the Holy Spirit have a joy within that must express itself. Singing and praising God is a natural outgrowth of this joy. For this reason, our singing does not depend on how we feel or on the circumstances around us. Instead, our singing depends on the indwelling ministry of the Spirit. How thrilling it is to be filled with the Spirit of God and to express that joy in singing psalms, hymns and spiritual songs!

In Ephesians 5:18 Paul made a contrast between

being filled with wine and being filled with the Spirit. A drunken person sometimes loses control and starts to sing; however, the Christian does not sing *out of control* but rather *out of His control*. When the Holy Spirit fills your heart with joy and fills your mind with God's truth, then you will want to express your joy in song.

Because of Sacrifice

As we have seen, those who have received Christ's gift of salvation, His holy Scriptures and His indwelling Spirit possess an inner joy that leads to singing. But Christians have another reason to sing that is not quite so easy to comprehend. We sing *because of sacrifice*.

How can sacrifice lead to singing? Throughout the Bible we find that when people were willing to give themselves completely to God, their sacrifice eventually led to blessing and joy. We can see this in the account of Abraham and Isaac in Genesis 22. Abraham was commanded by God to sacrifice his only son, Isaac, as a burnt offering. Abraham had placed his son on the altar and was about to plunge a knife into him when God intervened. In John 8:56 Christ stated that Abraham rejoiced to see His day, that is, the day of the Lord Jesus. When did that happen? When he sacrificed Isaac. Abraham saw in this act a picture of the Lord Jesus Christ, who died in mankind's place. Abraham's sacrifice of Isaac led to joy and singing.

Another example of this kind of sacrifice can be found in the story of Hannah (see I Sam. 1:1—2:11).

11

After waiting many years for a child, she entreated the Lord to bless her with a son. In return she promised to give him back to the Lord as His servant. The Lord kept His word, and she gave birth. Even though it was difficult to do, she remained faithful and gave her only son, Samuel, to the priest for him to raise. As she did, she burst forth in song (see 2:1-10). First came the sacrifice and then the song.

The New Testament also contains many examples of sacrifice and singing. When the angel spoke to Mary, telling her that she had been chosen to be the mother of the Messiah, she replied, "Behold the handmaid of the Lord; be it unto me according to thy word" (Luke 1:38). When Mary willingly presented her body as a living sacrifice, the joy she received in return caused her to burst forth into song: "My soul doth magnify the Lord, and my spirit hath rejoiced in God my Saviour" (vv. 46,47).

Often when a sacrifice is made, we do not see immediate or visible results. Many times it is hard to see any good in a difficult situation. But our reason for praising God should not be because of the blessings we expect to receive but because we have been given the opportunity to be a living sacrifice. When we have this kind of attitude, we can rejoice and sing even in the most difficult circumstances.

We can see this in the story of Paul and Silas in Acts 16:25. They had been beaten, humiliated, imprisoned and treated unjustly. Even though they believed that death was imminent, they could still sing because they were living sacrifices. Their reason for living was not to please themselves but rather to serve the Lord.

Sacrifice brings joy. Jesus told us that when we try to save our life, we will lose it. However, when we lose our life for the sake of the Lord Jesus, we will find it again (see Matt. 10:39). We glorify God as we surrender ourselves to Him. He, in turn, gives us a song in our hearts. The only Christian who does not have a song is the backslidden Christian. In Psalm 137 the Babylonians asked the Jews to sing them one of the songs of Zion. The Jewish people replied, "How shall we sing the Lord's song in a strange land?" (v. 4). These people had been living for themselves rather than for the Lord. As a result, they were in captivity. Their joy was gone, and therefore, they lost their song.

If you are backslidden and are living for the world rather than walking with God, then you will have no song *for* the Lord or *from* the Lord. But if you know the Lord and have experienced His salvation, if you are continually meditating on the Scriptures, if your heart is filled with the Spirit of God and if you have yielded yourself as a sacrifice, then you will have a new song that you can sing to the Lord because His joy fills your heart.

> *"O come, let us sing unto the Lord:*
> *Let us make a joyful noise to the rock of our salvation.*
> *Let us come before his presence with thanksgiving,*
> *And make a joyful noise unto him with psalms."*
> *(Ps. 95:1,2)*

Holy, Holy, Holy

Holy, Holy, Holy, Lord God Almighty!
Early in the morning our song shall rise to Thee;
Holy, Holy, Holy! Merciful and Mighty!
God in Three Persons, blessed Trinity!

Holy, Holy, Holy! All the saints adore Thee,
Casting down their golden crowns around the glassy sea;
Cherubim and seraphim falling down before Thee,
Which wert and art and evermore shalt be.

Holy, Holy, Holy! Tho the darkness hide Thee,
Tho the eye of sinful man Thy glory may not see;
Only Thou art holy—there is none beside Thee
Perfect in pow'r, in love and purity.

Holy, Holy, Holy, Lord God Almighty!
All Thy works shall praise Thy name in earth and sky and sea;
Holy, Holy, Holy! Merciful and Mighty!
God in Three Persons, blessed Trinity!

—Reginald Heber

Chapter 2

"Holy, Holy, Holy"

When you think of the Book of the Revelation, you automatically think of prophecy. But this book is much more than just a prediction of things to come. I have counted at least ten worship scenes in this book. Thus, we can learn a great deal about worship if we will listen to some of the hymns of praise recorded by the Apostle John in the Book of the Revelation.

The late Dr. A. W. Tozer once wrote: "I can safely say on the authority of all that is revealed in the Word of God that any man or woman on this earth who is bored and turned off by worship is not ready for heaven." I think Dr. Tozer was correct. Heaven is a place of worship, and if you and I cannot endure a time of worshiping God here on earth, what are we going to do when we get to heaven? Perhaps the greatest lack in our churches today is in the area of worship.

In Revelation 4 we find the basis for Bishop Reginald Heber's beloved worship hymn, "Holy, Holy, Holy." In this chapter the Apostle John is called up to heaven, and he relates what he sees: "And immediately I was in the spirit: and, behold, a throne

15

was set in heaven, and one sat on the throne. . . . And round about the throne were four and twenty seats: and upon the seats I saw four and twenty elders sitting, clothed in white raiment; and they had on their heads crowns of gold. . . . And round about the throne, were four beasts [living creatures] full of eyes before and behind. . . . And the four beasts had each of them six wings about him; and they were full of eyes within: and they rest not day and night, saying, Holy, holy, holy, Lord God Almighty, which was, and is, and is to come. And when those beasts give glory and honour and thanks to him that sat on the throne, who liveth for ever and ever, the four and twenty elders fall down before him that sat on the throne, and worship him that liveth for ever and ever, and cast their crowns before the throne, saying, Thou art worthy, O Lord, to receive glory and honour and power: for thou hast created all things, and for thy pleasure they are and were created" (vv. 2,4,6,8-11).

John's vivid description of this majestic scene in heaven reveals God and His glory to us. Like the elders in heaven, when we see God in all His glory through His Word, it should cause us to reverence and worship Him. Worship is essential, because the more we worship the Lord, the more we become like Him; and the more we become like Him, the more we please Him.

A Triune God

We find a description of many of God's attributes in Revelation 4. When we pause to reflect on these

16

qualities, then we, like the elders, will fall down in worship and adoration of our great God.

The first aspect of the Lord that we discover in this passage is that He is a triune God. In verse two we find God the Father seated on the throne. The Apostle John was "in the spirit," indicating the presence of the Holy Spirit. Then we read later that the Lamb is present in the midst of the throne (see 5:6). Thus, we have our triune God—God the Father (seated on the throne), God the Holy Spirit and God the Son. The Trinity is suggested, of course, by the repetition, "Holy, holy, holy" (4:8). The Prophet Isaiah witnessed a similar scene when he saw the Lord Jesus Christ on the throne. As he watched, he heard the seraphim say, "Holy, holy, holy, is the Lord of hosts: The whole earth is full of his glory" (Isa. 6:3).

We cannot explain the Trinity. We cannot demonstrate the reality of the triune God through the use of mathematics. We know there is one God, but this one God is found in three Persons—God the Father, God the Son and God the Holy Spirit. They are separate, and yet they are equal. Reginald Heber wrote the song "Holy, Holy, Holy" to commemorate Trinity Sunday on the church calendar. That's why he wrote: "Holy, Holy, Holy! Merciful and Mighty! / God in Three Persons, blessed Trinity!" All three Persons of the Trinity are involved in our salvation. We have been chosen by God the Father, purchased by God the Son and sealed by God the Holy Spirit. We belong to the triune God.

When we come to worship God, we worship the

17

Father through the Son and in the Holy Spirit. When we come to the house of God or to our private prayer closet, we must yield ourselves to the Holy Spirit and ask Him to "light the fire" on the altar of our heart to enable us to worship the Lord as we should.

A Sovereign God

We see God on His throne in Revelation 4, which causes us to realize that the God we worship is a sovereign God. The word "throne" is used 12 times in Revelation 4. In fact, it is used 46 times in the entire Book of the Revelation. God is on His throne; He has not abdicated His sovereign rule.

The Prophet Isaiah also saw a throne: "In the year that king Uzziah died I saw also the Lord sitting upon a throne, high and lifted up, and his train filled the temple" (Isa. 6:1). Isaiah saw the Lord Jesus Christ seated on the throne of glory.

The Apostle John recorded the fact that other thrones—24 of them—surrounded God's throne. The 24 elders were seated on these thrones. I believe these 24 elders represent God's people and that the number is a combination of the 12 tribes of Israel and the 12 apostles. Twenty-four was also the number of the priestly courses in the temple in the Old Testament.

Our sovereign God is the One who sits on the throne. But did you realize that we are enthroned with Him? When you were saved, Jesus Christ seated you with Himself in the heavenlies (see Eph.

18

2:6). You can hold no loftier position than to be seated with the sovereign God!

What does it mean that God is sovereign? It means that you will never find Him disturbed, worried or frustrated. Everything is under His control. Nothing catches Him by surprise. It also means that He does what He pleases, but we know that what He chooses to do is always right. He also possesses unlimited power. The living creatures call Him "Lord God Almighty" (Rev. 4:8). That name is used six times in the Book of the Revelation, while the name "Almighty" is used nine times. Probably no other book gives us such a clear picture of our sovereign God as the Book of the Revelation. Because He is sovereign, He also possesses the ability to be the Creator: "For thou hast created all things, and for thy pleasure they are and were created" (v. 11).

A Holy God

We not only worship a triune, sovereign God; but we also worship *a holy God.* The Lord's holiness is the focus of Bishop Heber's hymn. The word "holy" means "unique, set apart, separated, different." God is unique. Nothing else on earth or in heaven can be compared to Him.

One quality that sets Him apart is His purity. "God is light, and in him is no darkness at all" (I John 1:5). No sin, weakness or fault of any kind hinders God from being perfect, for He is pure.

We hear a great deal these days about the love of God, but we must keep in mind that His love is *holy.*

For this reason, He must deal drastically with sin. This explains why our Lord Jesus died on the cross—to uphold God's holiness and yet to reveal God's love. We are not saved by the love of God; we are saved by the grace of God. "For by grace are ye saved through faith" (Eph. 2:8). When we look at the grace of God, we see love that has paid a price. In order for the Lord to save us, He had to pay a price, because someone had to atone for our sins. The only One who could do it was the Lamb of God who was "slain from the foundation of the world" (Rev. 13:8).

An Eternal God

A fourth attribute of God that we see in Revelation 4 is that He is *eternal*. "Holy, holy, holy, Lord God Almighty, [who] was, and is, and is to come" (v. 8). You and I are not eternal. Anything that is eternal never had a beginning and will have no end. We all had a beginning. It is true that we are all immortal; that is, we are going to live forever somewhere—either in heaven or hell. We will have no end, but we all had a beginning when we were born.

Unlike us, God has existed forever. He had no beginning because He always was. This is something we humans cannot comprehend. If you try to conceive of God as eternal, you will probably end up with a headache!

Our God not only had no beginning and no end— He *is* the beginning and the end! "I am Alpha and Omega, the beginning and the ending, saith the

Lord" (1:8). "I Am" is one of God's names, and it refers to the fact that He is eternal. When Moses was being called by God to lead the Children of Israel out of Egypt, he said to God, "Tell me Your name" (see Ex. 3:13). God answered, "Thus shalt thou say unto the children of Israel, I Am hath sent me" (v. 14).

One way in which the Lord Jesus let the people know that He was truly God was by associating Himself with the I Am of the Old Testament. When He said, "I am the bread of life" (John 6:35) and "I am the good shepherd" (10:11), they understood that He was claiming to be deity.

When we worship God, we are in touch with eternity. This fact ought to make a difference in the way we use our time. I feel sorry for people who don't take time to worship God, because their lives don't have that glory, that touch, that special blessing of eternity. They are limited to time as they know it.

A Gracious God

One of the greatest attributes of the Lord, as far as humanity is concerned, is the fact that He is *a gracious God*. In Revelation 4:3 we are told that a rainbow surrounded the throne of God. You will remember that the rainbow was set apart in Genesis 9 to be the indication of God's faithfulness and grace. The Lord promised He would never again destroy the earth with a flood. When you see a rainbow in the clouds, you are reminded of this promise. However, the earth will be judged again;

only this time it will be with fire (see II Pet. 3:10-12).

The rainbow around the throne speaks of the grace of God. A rainbow is a beautiful bridge between heaven and earth. I recall once seeing a double rainbow after a storm. It was a magnificent sight, and it reminded me of the grace of God. Peter described God's grace as being "manifold" (I Pet. 4:10). That word "manifold" means "variegated" or "multicolored." We can see this grace in the 24 elders (who represent saved people) seated around the throne, wearing crowns of gold. I can understand the presence of angels, cherubim and seraphim in heaven, but *people*? This is only possible because we worship a gracious God.

I hope that one day you will be a part of that heavenly throng in white raiment, wearing the victor's crown of gold. Jesus Christ is the Author and Finisher of our faith (see Heb. 12:2). His sacrifice enables us to win the victory. Often in the Book of the Revelation we read the words: "To him that overcomes." Whoever believes that Jesus Christ is the Son of God is an overcomer (see I John 5:1-4). We win the victor's crown, not because of what we have done but because we have a holy and gracious God seated on the throne of grace.

A Faithful God

A sixth attribute of God we find in this passage is that He is *faithful*. We can see the Lord's faithfulness in His role as Creator. All things were made by Him and for Him. Not only has God created everything, including mankind, but He also lovingly cares

22

for and sustains it all. The elders' recognition of God's faithfulness caused them to fall down before Him in worship, exclaiming, "Thou art worthy, O Lord, to receive glory and honour and power" (Rev. 4:11).

Throughout the Scriptures we are reminded of God's great faithfulness. In the Old Testament we see God's continual protection of the Children of Israel. Despite their unfaithfulness, He kept His promise to bless them as His people. In the New Testament we see the Lord's faithfulness in His promises to us. He has promised never to leave us or forsake us (see Heb. 13:5). He will never allow us to be tempted beyond what we are able to resist (see I Cor. 10:13). When we fail, we have the assurance that "if we confess our sins, he is faithful and just to forgive us our sins, and to cleanse us from all unrighteousness" (I John 1:9). Because our God is faithful, we should worship Him in full assurance of our faith (see Heb. 10:22,23).

God, our Creator and Sustainer, is worthy of all our worship and praise. For this reason we should not neglect to give Him the honor and glory He so rightly deserves. When we worship, we must remember that the God we serve is triune (He is three Persons) and sovereign (He is seated on the throne of heaven). Our God is also holy and eternal. We could not approach His sovereign throne were it not for the blood of Jesus, whose sacrifice enables us to share eternal life with Him in heaven. Because our God is gracious, He has promised to clothe us in white and put a crown on our head. We can claim

23

this promise because the Lord is faithful—He always keeps His word. This knowledge should fill our minds and hearts completely as we worship our great God and Saviour. "O come, let us adore Him, Christ, the Lord"!

Does Jesus Care?

Does Jesus care when my heart is pained
Too deeply for mirth and song;
As the burdens press, and the cares distress,
And the way grows weary and long?

Does Jesus care when my way is dark
With a nameless dread and fear?
As the daylight fades into deep night shades,
Does He care enough to be near?

Does Jesus care when I've tried and failed
To resist some temptation strong;
When for my deep grief I find no relief,
Tho my tears flow all the night long?

Does Jesus care when I've said goodbye
To the dearest on earth to me,
And my sad heart aches till it nearly breaks—
Is it aught to Him? Does He see?

Chorus:
O yes, He cares—I know He cares!
His heart is touched with my grief;
When the days are weary, the long nights dreary,
I know my Savior cares.

—Frank E. Graeff

Chapter 3

"Does Jesus Care?"

Rev. Frank Graeff was a Methodist minister who served in the Philadelphia conference from 1890 until his death in 1919. Rev. Graeff was known as the "sunshine minister" because of his happy disposition and his optimistic faith. But at one time in his life he went through a very deep valley, and he lost his radiance and joy. He was a man full of defeat and despair. He was sure God had forsaken him. One day he began to sing, "What a Friend we have in Jesus, / All our sins and griefs to bear! / What a privilege to carry / Ev'rything to God in prayer!" That song caused him to fall on his knees and to seek the Lord in a new way. As he poured out his heart in prayer, Rev. Graeff felt God's peace flowing through him, and then he remembered I Peter 5:7: "Casting all your care upon him; for he careth for you." "I know He cares!" he shouted. "I know my Saviour cares!" As a result of that experience, he wrote the well-known song "Does Jesus Care?"

Whenever I sing this song, I often think of the account of Jesus' calming the storm (see Mark 4:35-41). The Lord and His disciples were crossing the Sea of Galilee when a terrible storm arose. The frightened men awakened Jesus and asked, "Master, carest thou not that we perish?" (v. 38). Like the disciples, I'm sure that every person has asked himself more than once in his life: *Does the Lord really care?*

Christians Have Cares

When we are at a low point in our lives, it becomes very easy to blame God and to doubt His care for us. At these times we, like Rev. Graeff, need to claim the Lord's promise: "Casting all your care upon him; for he careth for you" (I Pet. 5:7). This simple statement contains many wonderful encouragements that can help us weather the difficult and discouraging experiences we face.

The first encouragement we find in this passage is the fact that *Christians do have cares.* You may be saying to yourself, *This is no encouragement to me! I would rather hear you say that Christians* don't *have cares!* But I am encouraged to know that Peter acknowledged the fact that we, as God's children, do have cares and concerns.

I fear that many people today are promoting an unrealistic view of the Christian life. Certain media preachers, authors and songwriters are leading people to believe that the Christian life is one mountaintop experience after another. They try to convince us that once we become a Christian, we should have no burdens or problems in our life. If trials, pain, sickness or other difficulties arise, they argue, then something is wrong between you and God. We can see this type of thinking in the experience of Job. His friends argued that Job had to be a backslider; otherwise, God never would have permitted all those tragedies to take place. But we can see from the life of Job that the righteous *do* have valleys in their lives. We need to remember that in order to have mountaintops, we must also have valleys.

Because We Are Human

Why does the Lord sometimes lead us through the valley? I believe that there are three reasons why Christians have cares. First, we have cares *because we are human.* When we become a Christian, God does not suddenly take away our human nature. We must live with the same physical weaknesses that we experienced before we were saved.

Because we are human, it is only natural for us to have certain problems. When we are born into this world, we are very weak. We must depend totally on others for our care and sustenance. As we grow older, we learn how to handle life, how to walk and talk and how to feed and clothe ourselves. However, even at the prime of life, when our physical strength, mental ability and emotional zeal are at their height, we still face problems and difficult decisions.

Then at mid-life, we begin to reach a plateau. As we grow older and start that downward descent, the cares seem to increase. We are faced with even more physical, mental and emotional difficulties. However, the Lord doesn't take these problems away from us. Instead, He expects us to take care of

28

ourselves the best we can and trust Him to help us with the things we cannot handle. Because we are human and live in a human world, we cannot escape every care and trial in life. But we have Someone who can see us through these problems when we cast our cares on Him.

Because We Care About Others

Christians also have cares *because we care about others.* In this passage in I Peter 5, the apostle was especially addressing the spiritual leaders in the church. We read in verse 2: "Feed the flock of God which is among you, taking the oversight thereof." As Christians we are instructed to care for the needs of others. But caring often brings with it additional cares and concerns.

We can avoid a great many heartaches in this life by isolating ourselves from the rest of the world. If we refuse to talk to others, to become involved in Sunday school or church, to visit the sick and the grieving, to read or watch the news to see what is happening in the world or to listen to the announcements in church to find out who may be hurting, we can escape a great deal of suffering. But by ignoring the cares of others, we will also miss many blessings and will rob ourselves of the privilege of *being* a blessing.

Because We Have an Enemy

Christians have cares because we are human and because we are a caring people. We also have cares *because we have an enemy, the Devil.* In I Peter 5:8,

Peter went on to say, "Be sober, be vigilant; because your adversary the devil, as a roaring lion, walketh about, seeking whom he may devour."

Satan wants to see us fail in our Christian walk. For this reason, he often places cares and trials in our way in order to trip us up. We need to remember, however, that nothing can happen to the child of God apart from the will of God. With this warning in I Peter 5 also comes a promise: "But the God of all grace, who hath called us unto his eternal glory by Christ Jesus, after that ye have suffered a while, make you perfect, stablish, strengthen, settle you" (v. 10). God knows that we need to have cares and suffering. These trials help us to become mature, perfecting His work in our lives.

God Cares for Us

Christians have cares because we are a caring people who live in an imperfect world with an Enemy who is seeking to destroy us. Sometimes we may feel as if we are being crushed by our burdens; however, we need to remember that we are not alone. We can endure any care because of the fact that *God cares for us*.

How do we know God cares for us? Throughout the Word of God we have His *promises* to assure us that He cares. Nowhere is this more plainly stated than in I Peter 5:7: "Casting all your care upon him; for he careth for you." Because the Lord cares for us He has promised to provide for our physical needs (see Matt. 6:25-34), to give us a Helper to teach and comfort us (see John 14:16-18,26) and to give us peace for our emotionally troubled times (see v. 27). The Lord Jesus has assured us that He will take care of any need we have when we call on Him (see vv. 13,14). Therefore, we should not become anxious about our problems (see Phil. 4:6).

Not only do we have the Lord's promises, but His *providence* also proves that He cares. God is continually going before us and preparing the way. Nothing happens to the believer outside of the permissive, directive will of God. I'm encouraged to know that when I begin a new day, my Shepherd has already gone before me. One of the greatest assurances of God's providence is found in Romans 8:28: "And we know that all things work together for good to them that love God, to them who are the called according to his purpose."

The fact that He answers *prayer* is proof that He cares for us. Probably no one knew this fact better than the Apostle Peter. When Peter's mother-in-law was ill, Jesus healed her (see Luke 4:38,39). When he did not have the money to pay his taxes, the Lord enabled him to catch a fish that contained a coin for the tax (see Matt. 17:24-27). When Peter almost drowned one night, the Lord Jesus rescued him (see 14:25-31). When he lost his temper in the Garden of Gethsemane and almost killed a man, Christ healed the man's ear and saved Peter from arrest (see Luke 22:50,51). When the apostle was imprisoned, the Lord miraculously released him (see Acts 12:5-16). Then when Peter finally was martyred, Jesus Christ gave him the grace that he needed. Yes, Peter knew what he was talking about when he wrote: "Casting all your care upon him; for he careth for you" (I Pet. 5:7).

We Can Cast Our Cares on Him

Because we have the assurance that God cares for us, we also have the promise that *we can cast our cares on Him*, trusting Him to carry the burden for us. "Casting all your care upon him; for he careth for you" (I Pet. 5:7).

The word "care" in this passage could also be translated "anxiety." It means "being pulled apart." This is exactly what happens when you are facing a problem. Your mind says to you, *I know God cares for me*, but your hurting heart questions, *Where is the Lord?* You feel pulled apart. Peter is saying to you in this passage, "Give God your mind and your heart. Give the Lord *all* of your cares because He cares for you."

We don't cast our care on the Lord so that we can become careless, however. We give Him our cares so He can help us solve our problems and meet our needs. We are not talking about escaping responsibility but rather about the enablement that God can give to us if we will let Him.

Courage

When you cast all your cares on the Lord, what will He do for you? As you give your burdens to Him, He performs four very special ministries in your life.

32

First, He helps you by giving you the courage to face life unafraid. Isaiah 41:10 tells us, "Fear thou not; for I am with thee: be not dismayed; for I am thy God: I will strengthen thee; yea, I will help thee; yea, I will uphold thee with the right hand of my righteousness." When you cast all your care on the Lord, He gives you the courage to face life fearlessly and courageously. Instead of running from your problems, you can face them head-on and overcome them.

Wisdom

The second ministry the Lord performs in your life is that of giving you the wisdom to understand what He wants you to do. In James 1:5 we read: "If any of you lack wisdom, let him ask of God, that giveth to all men liberally, and upbraideth not; and it shall be given him." This promise was given within the context of suffering. In the preceding verses James exhorted, "My brethren, count it all joy when ye fall into divers [various] temptations; knowing this, that the trying of your faith worketh patience. But let patience have her perfect work, that ye may be perfect and entire, wanting nothing" (vv. 2-4).

How do we obtain this maturity? We mature in Christ as we learn patience through suffering. And having cares and concerns is part of that suffering. The Apostle Peter stated it well: "But the God of all grace, who hath called us unto his eternal glory by Christ Jesus, after that ye have suffered a while, make you perfect, stablish, strengthen, settle you" (I Pet. 5:10). When we have cares and do not know

33

what to do, we should ask God to grant us the wisdom we need for the situation.

Grace and Strength

The Lord gives us the courage to face our problems and the wisdom to understand them. He also gives us the grace and strength to do what we should. Philippians 4:13 states, "I can do all things through Christ which strengtheneth me." We often think that we only have the ability to handle the minor problems of life. When a major setback occurs, we fall apart. But this passage promises us that the Lord Jesus will give us the strength to do *all* things by His power. What a great promise to claim!

But we cannot be passive when it comes to fighting life's battles and solving our problems. Waiting on the Lord does not give us the right to be complacent and inactive. Waiting on the Lord involves preparing ourselves for what God wants us to do. Then He gives us the grace and strength to carry out His plan for solving that problem or facing that circumstance.

Faith

After we have been given the courage to face our cares, the wisdom to understand the situation and the grace and strength to act, the Lord performs one more special ministry in our lives. He gives us the *faith* to trust Him to do the rest.

Psalm 37:5 contains a wonderful promise: "Commit thy way unto the Lord; trust also in him; and he shall bring it to pass." When we have prayed for courage, wisdom and strength and have done every-thing the Lord has asked us to do, it is time to leave the problem in His hands. And we could not leave the situation in any better hands. The Hebrew word in this passage literally means to "roll thy way upon the Lord"; in other words, roll the burden off your back and onto the Lord's. Give Him your burdens and then wait. He will give you the faith to trust Him for the rest. When we have a problem, the worst thing we can do is to become impatient and impetu-ous, rushing ahead and doing what we think is best. This only leads to more problems.

Christians do have cares and do experience suf-fering. It is an inescapable part of life. But we belong to a God who cares. He has promised to take care of us, and what He has promised He is able to do. We can cast our cares on Him, trusting Him to give us the courage, wisdom, grace and strength to do what is required and to give us the faith to trust Him for the rest. Cast "all your care upon him; for he careth for you" (I Pet. 5:7).

All the Way My Savior Leads Me

All the way my Savior leads me—
What have I to ask beside?
Can I doubt His tender mercy,
Who thru life has been my Guide?
Heav'nly peace, divinest comfort,
Here by faith in Him to dwell!
For I know, whate'er befall me,
Jesus doeth all things well.

All the way my Savior leads me—
Cheers each winding path I tread,
Gives me grace for ev'ry trial,
Feeds me with the living bread.
Tho my weary steps may falter
And my soul athirst may be,
Gushing from the Rock before me,
Lo! a spring of joy I see.

All the way my Savior leads me—
O the fullness of His love!
Perfect rest to me is promised
In my Father's house above.
When my spirit, clothed immortal,
Wings its flight to realms of day,
This my song thru endless ages:
Jesus led me all the way.

—Fanny J. Crosby

Chapter 4

"All the Way My Savior Leads Me"

One day Fanny Crosby, the blind hymn writer, desperately needed five dollars. She took her need to the Lord in prayer. Soon a stranger came to her door and gave her the five dollars that she needed. As Fanny marveled at the Lord's leading, she began to praise Him for His goodness and provision. This experience led her to write the following words: "All the way my Savior leads me— / What have I to ask beside?"

This song is based on the experiences of the Israelites as they wandered through the wilderness. The unfaithful generation had died, and their children were preparing to enter the Promised Land. Just before his death, Moses spoke to the group, reminding them of what the Lord had done for their fathers and exhorting them to remain faithful: "All the commandments which I command thee this day shall ye observe to do, that ye may live, and multiply, and go in and possess the land which the Lord sware unto your fathers. And thou shalt remember all the way which the Lord thy God led thee these forty years in the wilderness, to humble thee, and to prove [test] thee, to know what was in thine heart, whether thou wouldest keep his commandments, or no. And he humbled thee, and suffered thee to hunger, and fed thee with manna, which thou knewest not, neither did thy fathers know; that he might make thee know that man doth not live by bread only, but by every word that proceedeth out of the mouth of the Lord doth man live. Thy raiment waxed not old upon thee, neither did thy foot swell, these forty years. Thou shalt also consider in thine heart that, as a man chasteneth his son, so the Lord thy God chasteneth thee" (Deut. 8:1-5).

The Book of Deuteronomy is the book of remembrance. At least 16 times in this book you find Moses using the word "remember." In addition, he used the word "forget" nine times in warning them of commands they should not forget. This new generation of Israelites had not been in Egypt when God's great miracles occurred. They had not witnessed the Lord's work in parting the Red Sea. This group needed to know what God had done for them during the past 40 years. They needed to remember the past.

I meet people today who want to wipe out the past. But the past has a rich heritage that we should not only appreciate but should also guard. While we must live in the present as we look forward to the future, it is good to occasionally walk in the old paths, remembering the way the Lord has led us in the past. By remembering the past, we can live in the present and look to the future with hope, trusting the Lord's leading in our lives.

The new generation had a new leader—Joshua. They were facing a new challenge—conquering the land. Along with this challenge came a new peril—*success*. Once they settled in the land and became prosperous, they might forget what the Lord had done for them and turn away from following Him. We read later, in the Book of Judges, that the people did this very thing.

Whenever we are involved in a new endeavor, it is often easy for us to take credit for our success, forgetting the Lord's help along the way. For this reason, it is important to remember not only our past experiences but also the experiences of others. Thus, we can learn a great deal from the example of the Israelites. By remembering their choices, we can possibly avoid repeating the same mistakes: "Now these things were our examples, to the intent we should not lust after evil things, as they also lusted" (I Cor. 10:6). This is one reason why the Scriptures have been given to us. Another reason can be found in Romans 15:4: "For whatsoever things were written aforetime were written for our learning, that we through patience and comfort of the scriptures might have hope."

God Has a Way for Us to Walk

The Israelites' pilgrim journey in the wilderness not only points out the mistakes we should avoid, but it also offers us encouragement for our Christian walk. In Deuteronomy 8:2 we find three assurances of the Lord's leading and protection in our lives. When we lay hold of these promises, we can

39

have comfort, peace and hope even in the most troubled times.

The first assurance we find in this passage is that *God has a way for each of us to walk*. While the Lord has laid out in His Word a general road for us to follow, He also has a *specific* path for every individual to walk. I firmly believe that my Father in heaven does not hand me a road map that was drawn for someone else. He gives me directions that were designed especially for me.

The fact that God has a specific plan for each person's life can be seen by looking at our birth. According to Psalm 139, when I was conceived in my mother's womb, God had already designed my genetic structure. Before I was even born, the Lord had already determined how I would look, what talents I would possess and what direction my life would take. God arranged a long time ago that I would not be a professional football player or a mechanic. From the moment of conception the Lord gives each person everything he will need in order to walk in the specific path that He has planned for him.

Our salvation also proves that the Lord has a specific way for each one of us to walk. We read in Ephesians 2:10: "For we are his workmanship, created in Christ Jesus unto good works, which God hath before ordained that we should walk in them." The word "ordained" in this passage literally means "prepared." God has prepared works for each of us to fulfill. If we are walking in His path, we will perform the works that He has called us to do.

Not only do our physical birth and our new birth demonstrate God's plan for every believer, but this can also be seen in the variety of spiritual gifts given to Christians. If the Lord expected every person to perform the same job, then He would not have given us different spiritual gifts. The Lord has given to some the ability to teach and preach, while others have the gifts of evangelism or administration. This variety permits the Body to function properly, as well as allowing each person to fulfill the ministry God has planned for him.

God Has a Purpose for What Happens

Since the Lord has a specific way for each of us to walk, we can also be assured that *He has a purpose for everything that happens.* Moses reminded the Israelites that they had been forced to wander in the wilderness for a special reason. Deuteronomy 8:2 tells us what that purpose was: "And thou shalt remember all the way which the Lord thy God led thee these forty years in the wilderness, to humble thee, and to prove thee, to know what was in thine heart, whether thou wouldest keep his commandments or no."

The Israelites' wilderness experience was a time of *testing.* After the Lord powerfully led the people out of Egypt and parted the Red Sea for them, He allowed their food and water supplies to be depleted and the Amalekites to attack them in order to test their faith in Him. Many times they failed the test. They complained bitterly about their lack of food and water and, on a number of occasions, con-

41

sidered returning to Egypt. They soon forgot the Lord's past protection and guidance.

In addition to testing them, the Lord allowed the wilderness experience as a time of *teaching*. The Israelites learned much about the character of God in the wilderness. They saw His mighty power displayed again and again, as well as His great faithfulness in caring for them. While they were in the wilderness, the Lord gave them the Law, teaching them what they needed to do to follow Him. He also revealed His plan for the nation of Israel to them. Psalm 103:7 tells us that "He made known his ways unto Moses, his acts unto the children of Israel." Day by day the Lord was showing the people that they could depend on His word. They needed to learn that "man doth not live by bread only, but by every word that proceedeth out of the mouth of the Lord" (Deut. 8:3).

Besides teaching the people to rely on His word, the Lord allowed them to go through these circumstances so that they might know what was in their hearts. The people did not realize that trouble was brewing in their hearts. They had not learned yet that "the heart is deceitful above all things and desperately wicked: who can know it?" (Jer. 17:9). But God knew their evil thoughts and desires and allowed them to experience difficulty in order to remind them of their sinful nature.

In allowing the people to be tested, the Lord not only wanted to teach them but He also wanted their wilderness experience to be a time of *trusting*. The people needed to learn to lean on the Lord rather than trusting in their own power. In order to do this, they first had to be humbled. These trials and experiences taught the Israelites that they could not find their way to the Promised Land or fight their enemies alone. They discovered that they needed the Lord's provision and guidance: "And he humbled thee, and suffered thee to hunger, and fed thee with manna" (Deut. 8:3).

The Lord often allows us to be tested for these very same reasons. Many times He uses suffering and difficulties as a means of teaching us and of humbling us so we will learn to trust in Him. God wants us to walk by faith and not by sight. We need to learn to depend on His Word and to trust Him to take care of us. If you are experiencing a time of testing, remember, the Lord has a purpose for everything that happens to you. Seek to discover what the Lord is trying to teach you in that experience, and trust Him to see you through it.

God Will Guide Us on Our Way

The Lord has designed a specific plan for our lives. Everything that happens to us falls within that plan and purpose. For this reason, we can always be assured that *God will guide us on our way:* "Thou shalt remember all the way which the Lord thy God led thee" (Deut. 8:2). We can also be assured that the Lord will not desert us somewhere along the path but will see us through to the end.

Like the Israelites, many times we rebel against the Lord's leading and stray from the path. During these times it often becomes necessary for Him to

43

chasten us in order to lead us back to the right path. When we are being punished, we often think that God has left us alone, not realizing that this trial has been given to us for our own good.

Since the Lord has a specific plan for each of us and a purpose in our experiences, we can be certain that He will reveal His will to us. We can also rely on Him to help us make decisions that affect our lives.

Many people today are asking the question "How can I know the Lord's will for my life?" They look for specific and miraculous signs, such as the ones that the Lord gave to the Israelites. But God doesn't give us a pillar of fire in the sky to follow. Instead, He gives us an even greater light for our lives—the Word of God. "Thy word is a lamp unto my feet, and a light unto my path" (Ps. 119:105). Just as the Lord spoke to the Israelites through the pillar of cloud (see 99:7), He speaks to us today through His Word. We must remember, however, that we cannot take every word spoken to Moses and others in the Bible and apply it literally to our lives. God has never commanded us to smite a rock or walk through a river. These were directions given to Moses for a specific purpose. But we can learn from the teachings given to Moses because *all* Scripture is profitable (see II Tim. 3:16,17). When we open our Bible, God opens His lips and speaks to us. The Lord guides us on our journey by His Word.

Of course, it is important that we use our common sense as we make decisions in life. In seeking the Lord's will, it is vital that we know ourselves and evaluate the circumstances. The Lord is not going to send us a telegram, telling us what to do. Instead, He gives us the wisdom to make decisions that are within His will.

It is also vital that we seek godly counsel and pray for the Holy Spirit's direction in our lives. I firmly believe that those who truly *want* to know the will of God can know it (see John 17:17). If you don't know what the Lord wants you to do, just wait on Him. At the right time He will reveal His will to you.

Throughout the Old Testament we can see the Lord's leading and protection in the lives of the Israelites. God did not forsake them, and He will not forsake us. He has promised to lead us along the path that He has planned just for us. Because the Lord has a way for us to walk, we can be assured that He also has a purpose in everything that happens. He uses these experiences to test us and teach us so that we can learn to trust Him more. We can trust Him to guide us every step of the way on our journey through life. As we claim these assurances, we can then say with Fanny Crosby, "All the way my Savior leads me— / What have I to ask beside?"

God has brought you this far. He is not going to forsake you now! The Lord will continue to lead you because He always finishes what He starts. He is the Alpha and Omega, the beginning and the end (see Rev. 22:13). Keep your eyes on Him, trust Him, and He will open the way for you.

To God Be the Glory

To God be the glory—great things He hath done!
So loved He the world that He gave us His Son,
Who yielded His life an atonement for sin
And opened the Lifegate that all may go in.

O perfect redemption, the purchase of blood!
To ev'ry believer the promise of God;
The vilest offender who truly believes,
That moment from Jesus a pardon receives.

Great things He hath taught us, great things He hath done,
And great our rejoicing thru Jesus the Son;
But purer and higher and greater will be
Our wonder, our transport, when Jesus we see.

Chorus:
Praise the Lord, Praise the Lord,
Let the earth hear His voice!
Praise the Lord, Praise the Lord,
Let the people rejoice!
O come to the Father thru Jesus the Son,
And give Him the glory—great things He hath done.

—Fanny J. Crosby

Chapter 5

"To God Be the Glory"

When I was a lad growing up in Sunday school and church, I don't recall ever singing "To God Be the Glory." Yet Fanny Crosby published this song back in 1875. It was almost 75 years before this hymn caught on in the United States, but it was popular in Great Britain for many years before that. Ira Sankey used this song in the Moody crusades and published it in his popular book, *Sacred Songs and Solos*. Then after a period of declining popularity, "To God Be the Glory" was reintroduced in Great Britain at Billy Graham's Herringay crusade in 1954. From there it came back to the United States, the country of its origin, where it was published in the *Nashville Crusade Hymnbook*. Today, this song is a favorite with congregations everywhere. "To God be the glory—great things He hath done!"

I am grateful that this song has been rediscovered. We need to be reminded constantly that we worship and serve a great God. Nothing is too hard for Him. Sometimes you and I are like the Jewish spies who were sent into the Promised Land to survey the situation. On their return ten of them warned the others, "The people are as tall as giants! We are like grasshoppers compared to them! We cannot conquer this land!" (see Num. 13:26-33). These men did not lift their eyes high enough. But Joshua and Caleb, the two faithful spies, replied, "We are perfectly able to go in and take the land because our God is a great God."

We need to remember that the God we serve is all-powerful. He is greater than any problem we may have. He is greater than our enemies: "Greater is he that is in you, than he that is in the world" (I John 4:4). If you are feeling discouraged and defeated, perhaps you need to be reminded once again of all that the Lord has done for you. When you pause to reflect on these blessings, then you can say with Fanny Crosby, "To God be the glory—great things He hath done!"

He Is Greater Than Our Future

We can see God's greatness in many areas of our life. Let's examine seven aspects of His greatness through the witness of several prominent Bible characters. First, in the life of Moses we see that *He is greater than our future*.

Throughout the Book of Deuteronomy, Moses continually reminded the Israelites of what the Lord had done for them in the past in bringing them out of Egypt. In chapter 10 Moses was instructing the new generation as they were preparing to enter the land of Canaan. In describing the wonderful miracles that God had performed in their journey between Egypt and Canaan, Moses concluded by saying,

"He is thy praise, and he is thy God, that hath done for thee these great and terrible [awesome] things, which thine eyes have seen" (v. 21).

Many of the people were fearful about their future. In order to claim the Promised Land they first would have to fight many fierce battles and conquer many strong enemies. Because of their fathers' lack of faith, they had been forced to wander in the wilderness for 40 years. Moses exhorted the Israelites to trust God and remain faithful to Him. If they faithfully kept His commandments, then the Lord would make them greater than any enemy they would face (see 11:22-25).

Like the Israelites, we often worry about our future, forgetting everything that God has done for us in the past. Since God has proved that He is greater than our past problems, we can be certain that He is also greater than our future ones. Rather than worrying about finances, health, job and other responsibilities, give them to God and trust Him to take care of them. Remember, *God is able!* Our God is a great God, and He does great things.

He Is Greater Than Our Bad Decisions

Not only is God greater than any problems we might face in the future, but also *He is greater than any bad decisions* we may make in the present. We can see this truth in the example of the Jewish people who lived during the time of the Prophet Samuel.

Many times in the Old Testament we find the

49

Israelites falling away from God. They often rebelled against the Lord by worshiping the heathen gods of the people around them. As a result, God allowed them to be conquered by other nations. This was true in the Book of Judges. But each time the Lord would eventually deliver the Children of Israel from their enemies by sending a judge to lead them.

In I Samuel we find the Israelites once again trying to imitate the heathen nations around them. They asked God to give them a king to lead them so they could be like the other countries. Samuel grieved over their decision, for he realized that they were, in effect, rejecting the Lord's rule. But God told Samuel that He would give the people what they wanted, even though their decision would eventually cause them trouble and heartache (see 8:6-22). In anointing Saul to be king, Samuel exhorted the people, saying, "Only fear the Lord, and serve him in truth with all your heart: for consider how great things he hath done for you" (12:24).

Samuel warned the Israelites of the consequences of their bad decision. With the warning the prophet also gave them the Lord's promise: "For the Lord will not forsake his people for his great name's sake: because it hath pleased the Lord to make you his people" (v. 22). Even though King Saul caused the nation of Israel many problems, the Lord eventually turned their bad decision into a blessing in the person of King David. Through David and his descendants, Jesus—the King of kings—came into the world.

When you make a bad decision and find yourself

losing God's blessing, you can always come back and start over again. Our great God has promised never to leave us or forsake us. We can come to Him in repentance and receive forgiveness for our mistakes. When we fear the Lord and seek to follow Him, He will take even our bad decisions and turn them into blessings.

He Is Greater Than Our Plans

The life and witness of David shows us another important aspect of God's greatness: *He is greater than our plans.* King David had made great plans to build a magnificent house of worship for the Lord. The king told Nathan, a prophet, "See now, I dwell in an house of cedar, but the ark of God dwelleth within curtains" (II Sam. 7:2). David reasoned that it was wrong for him to live in a beautiful house while the people were still worshiping God in the tabernacle, a tent built while the Israelites were wandering in the wilderness.

While David's intentions were good and his plans were noble, the Lord had something even better in mind for him. God told David that He did not want him to build a house (the temple); however, his son would be allowed to do it (*see* vv. 12,13; I Kings 5:5). Instead of David's building a house for God, the Lord planned to build the "house" of David: "And thine house and thy kingdom shall be established for ever before thee: thy throne shall be established for ever" (I Sam. 7:16). This is a reference to the birth of the Messiah, who would reign for eternity.

The Lord chose David and his descendants to be

the family from whom the Saviour would come. What an honor and privilege was given to David! While his plan would have only brought temporary honor and blessing to God and to himself, God's plan for David brought eternal blessings to the entire world. As the king pondered the greatness of God and His plan, he praised Him, saying, "For thy word's sake, and according to thine own heart, hast thou done all these great things, to make thy servant know them. Wherefore thou art great, O Lord God: for there is none like thee, neither is there any God beside thee, according to all that we have heard with our ears. And what one nation in the earth is like thy people, even like Israel, whom God went to redeem for a people to himself, and to make him a name, and to do for you great things and terrible, for thy land, before thy people, which thou redeemedst to thee from Egypt, from the nations and their gods?" (II Sam. 7:21-23). David bore witness that our God is greater than any plan man can devise.

God has great things planned for each of us. But often we are so busy making and carrying out our own plans that we ignore what the Lord wants us to do. As a result, we miss out on the blessings that He wants to give us. We need to be open to the Lord's leading so that He can reveal His plan for our lives to us. Like David, often God's plan for us is fulfilled in the lives of our children and grandchildren. Therefore, it is important that we pray for our offspring. Many years ago one of my ancestors prayed that each generation of our family would have someone who would be a minister of the Gospel. His prayer has been answered to this day.

If it seems that all your plans and dreams are being shattered, don't despair! The Lord has a plan for your life. Trust Him to reveal His will to you in His perfect timing. His plans are greater than yours!

He Is Greater Than Our Thoughts

We learn another important truth about God and His greatness from the story of Job. His experience teaches us that we cannot comprehend the mind and purposes of the Lord, for *He is greater than our thoughts.*

Job was a very righteous man, and the Lord had blessed him greatly. But then Satan asked for and obtained permission to test him. He destroyed Job's family and possessions and caused him to break out in painful boils. As this suffering man sat in an ash heap, three of his friends came to offer their condolences (and explanations) to him. These men thought they knew the Lord's purpose for Job's plight: they accused him of committing some great sin. They believed that God never allowed the righteous to suffer.

Then a fourth friend, Elihu, offered his advice to Job. Even though Elihu's explanation of God's purpose was also wrong, he did understand one very important truth about the Lord. He stated, "God thundereth marvellously with his voice; great things doeth he, which we cannot comprehend" (Job 37:5).

Job and his friends learned that just as we do not

understand how God created the world and how He sustains everything in it, we cannot know the mind and purposes of the Lord. Isaiah 55:8,9 states, "For my thoughts are not your thoughts, neither are your ways my ways, saith the Lord. For as the heavens are higher than the earth, so are my ways higher than your ways, and my thoughts than your thoughts."

God does great things that we cannot comprehend. The Lord's mind is much greater than ours; therefore, we should not try to explain His ways. Remember, we do not live on explanations; we live on promises. Even though the height and depth of the Lord's plan is beyond our understanding, we can still know that He is working in our behalf. Thus, we do not need to have great knowledge— only great faith.

He Is Greater Than Our Human Limitations

Not only is God greater than our thoughts, our decisions and our plans, but *He is also greater than our human limitations*. Many times we feel as if we are facing impossible obstacles and are being asked to perform tasks that are too great for us. But we need to remember that no task is too great for God. He can work miracles in our lives, if we will only submit to His power.

One of the greatest examples of the Lord's power can be seen in the life of Mary, the mother of Jesus Christ. God performed a miracle in her life through the power of His Holy Spirit. Even though she was a virgin, she conceived and bore the most precious

54

baby of all—the Lord Jesus Christ. Although Mary could not understand the miracle that God was performing, she willingly submitted to His plan for her (see Luke 1:26-38). Mary's realization of God's power over her humanness caused her to sing a song of praise to Him: "My soul doth magnify the Lord, and my spirit hath rejoiced in God my Saviour. For he hath regarded the low estate of his handmaiden: for, behold, from henceforth all generations shall call me blessed. For he that is mighty hath done to me great things; and holy is his name" (vv. 46-49).

God took an ordinary young woman and used her for His greatest miracle. No person is too small for God to use, and no job is too big for the Lord to perform. You can rely on the Lord's promise in Philippians 4:13: "I can do all things through Christ which strengtheneth me." God is greater than your human limitations. He can make your life a miracle, if you will only yield to Him.

He Is Greater Than the Powers of Darkness

We find a sixth important aspect of God's greatness in the story of the demoniac in Mark 5. Christ's healing of this demon-possessed man shows us that *He is greater than the powers of darkness.*

Jesus and the disciples had just stepped out of their boat after crossing the Sea of Galilee when they saw a man who was possessed by many demons. The man lived like an animal among the tombs. The Lord cast out the demons, and they entered a herd of swine, causing the animals to race over a cliff and into the sea where they were drowned (see vv. 1-13). The man was so grateful to Christ for delivering him from his agony and shame that he wanted to go with the Lord Jesus. But this was not the Lord's will for him. Jesus told the man, "Go home to thy friends, and tell them how great things the Lord hath done for thee, and hath had compassion on thee" (v. 19).

Christ has delivered us from the darkness of sin and death through His redemption on the cross (see Col. 1:13,14). Satan's powers have no hold on us because "greater is he that is in you, than he that is in the world" (I John 4:4). Just as the demons fled from the presence of Jesus, the power of Christ in us will cause Satan to flee when we resist him (see James 4:7). We can live victoriously in a world filled with darkness when we are submitted to Christ, the Light of the world. When we think about the freedom that we enjoy in the Lord Jesus, we should desire to tell others about the great things He has done in our lives.

He Is Greater Than Our Enemies

Throughout the Old Testament we find the Lord continually delivering the Children of Israel from their enemies. While we may not be in captivity to other nations, Christians today still face many enemies who are trying to destroy their faith. But we do not have to be afraid because *God is greater than our enemies*, and He will deliver us.

In Psalm 126 the psalmist spoke of the great things that the Lord had done in delivering the
56

Children of Israel from captivity: "When the Lord turned again the captivity of Zion, we were like them that dream. Then was our mouth filled with laughter, and our tongue with singing: then said they among the heathen, The Lord hath done great things for them. The Lord hath done great things for us; whereof we are glad" (vv. 1-3).

This psalm, I believe, is not talking about Judah's deliverance from the Babylonian Captivity but rather their deliverance from the Assyrian invasion (see II Kings 18,19). The armies of Sennacherib had gathered around Jerusalem (Zion) and were trying to starve the people so they could capture the city. King Hezekiah prayed fervently to the Lord. The Lord heard his prayer and sent Isaiah to the king to tell him of the coming deliverance. That same night an angel of the Lord entered the Assyrians' camp and killed 185,000 enemy soldiers (see 19:8-35; Isa. 36,37). This all happened so suddenly and in such a marvelous way that even the Gentile nations said, "The Lord hath done great things for them" (Ps. 126:2). Then the Jewish people responded, "The Lord hath done great things for us; whereof we are glad" (v. 3).

He Deserves the Glory

We have a great God who has done great things for us. We can live confidently in a troubled world because our God is greater than our enemies and the powers of darkness that seek to control us. When we make bad decisions, He is great enough to forgive and to help us overcome them. His thoughts are much higher than our own, and He has plans for our lives that are greater than any we could imagine or devise. He is greater than our human limitations and can work miracles in our lives if we will let Him. We can look to the future with hope because the Lord is in control of our destiny.

Because our Lord has done such great things for us, He deserves all the glory and honor we can give to Him. Psalm 29:1,2 tells us, "Give unto the Lord, O ye mighty, give unto the Lord glory and strength. Give unto the Lord the glory due unto his name; worship the Lord in the beauty of holiness."

As Fanny Crosby considered the salvation she had received in Christ, her heart was filled with thanksgiving and awe for His greatness and mercy. She responded in praise to God, saying, "To God be the glory—great things He hath done." If you have not been giving the Lord the glory He deserves, perhaps you have not been dwelling enough on the blessings you have received from Him.

The Lord has given us many wonderful gifts, and He will continue to do great things for us as we trust and praise Him with our hearts, lips and lives. "To God be the glory—great things He hath done."

How Firm a Foundation

How firm a foundation, ye saints of the Lord,
Is laid for your faith in His excellent Word!
What more can He say than to you He hath said—
To you, who for refuge to Jesus have fled?

"Fear not, I am with thee—O be not dismayed,
For I am thy God, I will still give thee aid;
I'll strengthen thee, help thee, and cause thee to stand,
Upheld by my gracious, omnipotent hand."

"When thru the deep waters I call thee to go,
The rivers of woe shall not thee overflow;
For I will be with thee thy troubles to bless,
And sanctify to thee thy deepest distress."

"When thru fiery trials thy pathway shall lie,
My grace, all-sufficient, shall be thy supply;
The flame shall not hurt thee—I only design
Thy dross to consume and thy gold to refine."

"The soul that on Jesus hath leaned for repose,
I will not, I will not desert to his foes;
That soul, tho all hell should endeavor to shake,
I'll never—no, never—no, never forsake!"

Chapter 6

"How Firm a Foundation"

When President Andrew Jackson was dying, he asked the friends gathered around his bed to sing "How Firm a Foundation" for him. Robert E. Lee, who was a devout Christian, requested that this song be sung at his funeral. I have conducted many funeral services in my pastoral ministry, but I cannot recall ever using "How Firm a Foundation" in a service. Yet it is a song that is good to sing in times of sorrow and trial, as well as in times of triumph. This is one of the most biblical songs in our hymnbook, and yet we do not even know who wrote these marvelous words!

> How firm a foundation, ye saints of the Lord,
> Is laid for your faith in His excellent Word!
> What more can He say than to you He hath said—
> To you, who for refuge to Jesus have fled?

The first verse of this song is based on Hebrews 6:18: "That by two immutable things, in which it was impossible for God to lie, we might have a strong consolation, who have fled for refuge to lay hold upon the hope set before us." In this passage we are told that our lives are built on two unchangeable foundations—Jesus Christ, our hope and refuge, and His Word.

If your life is built on the foundation of the Word of God, then you can have strength and courage to face anything. When you trust in the Lord Jesus Christ, you receive more than just the gift of eternal life. He becomes the strength of your life and a refuge in times of trouble. When you call on Him, He is always there to help: "I waited patiently for the Lord; and he inclined unto me, and heard my cry. He brought me up also out of an horrible pit, out of the miry clay, and set my feet upon a rock, and established my goings. And he hath put a new song in my mouth, even praise unto our God" (Ps. 40:1-3).

I hope that your Christian life is built on the Word of God—not on some secondhand ideas from people but on your firsthand reading and understanding of the Word. If your life is built on something other than God's Word, you are building on shifting sand, and your foundation will crumble. That is why it is so important to read the Bible daily—to meditate on it, to study it and to learn what it says about God. For the more you know the Word of God, the more you will know the God of the Word, and the stronger the foundation under your feet will be.

In my counseling ministry I have sometimes said to people, "Exactly what would you want God to do or say to you to solve your problem? If God could walk into this hospital room right now and say something to you, what would you want Him to say?" People usually respond, "Well, Brother Wiersbe, I don't really know." Then I will usually reply, "My guess is that He would say something to you that He has already said in His Word."

Many people today make the mistake of seeking visions or new revelations from God. They want the Lord to speak to them directly, telling them what to do. But Jesus told us that we should not seek after signs: "An evil and adulterous generation seeketh after a sign; and there shall no sign be given to it, but the sign of the prophet Jonas: for as Jonas was three days and three nights in the whale's belly; so shall the Son of man be three days and three nights in the heart of the earth" (Matt. 12:39,40; see also 16:4; Mark 8:12; Luke 11:29,30).

Christ's resurrection from the dead was the greatest miracle ever performed. This sign has enabled us not only to receive salvation but also to know that everything He has told us in His Word is true. The Bible is God's final and complete revelation. "What more can He say than to you He hath said?" It's all been said, and Jesus Christ is God's last Word (see John 1:1; Heb. 1:1,2).

In Spite of Feelings

When you are trusting the Word of God and relying on the God of the Word, then you can face anything. Your foundation is firm *in spite of your feelings.* The second verse of "How Firm a Foundation" talks about your feelings:

"Fear not, I am with thee—O be not dismayed,
For I am thy God, I will still give thee aid;
I'll strengthen thee, help thee, and cause thee to stand,
Upheld by my gracious, omnipotent hand."

We find the basis for this verse in Isaiah 41:10: "Fear thou not; for I am with thee: be not dismayed; for I am thy God: I will strengthen thee; yea, I will help thee; yea, I will uphold thee with the right hand of my righteousness."

Fear is a real problem today. Some people are afraid to go to the doctor because they fear that he will discover a serious problem. Other people do not read the newspaper or watch TV because they fear what is happening in the world. Many are afraid to "get involved" and help those in need because of their fear that the person will swindle or harm them. People are being shackled and paralyzed by their fear of the past, present and future. They worry that the past will catch up with them, that they will not be able to cope with their present life and that the future will hold even more problems for them. Yet time and time again God tells us in His Word, "Fear not, for I am with you."

When your life is grounded in Christ and His Word, then your foundation will be firm, in spite of your feelings. In Isaiah 41:10 notice what God says: "I am . . . I will." In the Bible the words "I am" are always used in reference to God. The Lord gave Himself this name when speaking to Moses on Mount Horeb. When Moses asked God whom he should say had sent him, the Lord replied, "I Am

63

That I Am: . . . Thus shalt thou say unto the children of Israel, I Am hath sent me unto you" (Ex. 3:14). In the Book of Isaiah the Lord again affirms who He is—"For I am thy God" (41:10). He also assures us with the words "I am with thee: be not dismayed" (v. 10). Because God is the great I Am, He can say "I will"—"I will strengthen thee; yea, I will help thee; yea, I will uphold thee with the right hand of my righteousness" (v. 10).

Even when the world is falling apart around us, we do not need to worry. Our Lord has promised to be with us, to give us strength and to protect us. He will not fail us.

In Spite of Circumstances

When we base our Christian life solidly on God's Word, then our foundation will be firm in spite of feelings of fear or doubt. Even when we are experiencing difficulties, our foundation will remain firm *in spite of our circumstances.* The third and fourth stanzas of "How Firm a Foundation" describe those times when we must pass through the deep waters of sorrow and troubles or be tested by fiery trials:

> "When thru the deep waters I call thee to go,
> The rivers of woe shall not thee overflow;
> For I will be with thee thy troubles to bless,
> And sanctify to thee thy deepest distress."

> "When thru fiery trials thy pathway shall lie,
> My grace, all-sufficient, shall be thy supply;
> The flame shall not hurt thee—I only design
> Thy dross to consume and thy gold to refine."

These verses are based on Isaiah 43:2: "When thou passest through the waters, I will be with thee; and through the rivers, they shall not overflow thee; when thou walkest through the fire, thou shalt not be burned; neither shall the flame kindle upon thee." When we are feeling the pain of sorrow or troubles, we can rest in the knowledge that God is greater than our circumstances. He will not allow us to be overcome by them.

Notice, however, that God never promises to spare us from trials. Instead, He assures us that He will be with us as we pass through the deep waters and fires of life. But many people today are preaching a brand of theology that tries to convince us Christians should never go through difficult circumstances. If we are experiencing sickness, financial troubles or a death in the family, then something is wrong in our Christian life, they tell us. This is the argument that Job's friends presented to him. They said, "Job, if you were a godly man, you would not have lost all your wealth. Your children would not have died, and you wouldn't be sick right now." Then at the end of the Book of Job, God spoke to Job, telling him that just as man doesn't understand how the Lord sustains the universe, he cannot comprehend the mind and purposes of the Creator.

Every person will pass through deep waters at some time. When we do, we need to remember that God is the One who has called us to go through them because He has a wonderful purpose in mind: "For I will be with thee thy troubles to bless." The unsaved people of this world cannot understand

65

how we can receive a blessing from sorrow and troubles. When they are facing some difficulty in life, they wonder *how* they can get out of it. On the other hand, when Christians experience severe problems, they wonder *what* they can get out of it. We can do this because of the Lord's assurance that He will be with us in our sorrows so they will not "overflow." We rely on God's promise that "all things work together for good to them that love God" (Rom. 8:28).

Why do Christians experience fiery trials? God allows them in order to test and prove our faith. I Peter 1:7 states, "That the trial of your faith, being much more precious than of gold that perisheth, though it be tried with fire, might be found unto praise and honour and glory at the appearing of Jesus Christ." The Book of James tells us that the testing of our faith produces patience and endurance, perfecting our Christian life so we will be complete. Thus, we can have joy in the midst of trials (see 1:2-4).

The Apostle Paul faced many trials in his life. He was beaten, imprisoned and ridiculed for his faith. In addition, he faced some severe health problems. Paul prayed three times for healing, but God chose not to heal him. The Lord told him, "My grace is sufficient for thee: for my strength is made perfect in weakness" (II Cor. 12:9). God had a purpose in Paul's suffering—to help him be submissive so that He could work in and through him. Paul realized that his "thorn in the flesh" (see v. 7) was really a blessing in disguise. He was then able to say, "Therefore I take pleasure in infirmities, in reproaches, in necessities, in persecutions, in distresses for Christ's sake: for when I am weak, then am I strong" (v. 10).

Not only does God work *in spite of* our circumstances, but He also works *through* our circumstances. If the Lord has been calling you to walk through the fire, rejoice in the opportunity. God has given us sorrows in order to bless us and trials in order to test and perfect us. Along with the trials, He has promised to give us grace that is sufficient enough for any problem we face.

In Spite of Aging

It's interesting to note that the original version of "How Firm a Foundation" contains a verse that is not found in many modern hymnbooks. The older I get, the more I appreciate the words of this stanza:

> "E'en down to old age all My people shall prove
> My sovereign, eternal, unchangeable love;
> And then, when grey hairs shall their temples adorn,
> Like lambs they shall still in My bosom be borne."

Once again, this verse has been taken out of one of the great promises found in the Book of Isaiah: "And even to your old age I am he; and even to hoar [gray] hairs will I carry you: I have made, and I will bear; even I will carry, and will deliver you" (46:4). The setting of this verse is a message that Isaiah gave to the Israelites, exhorting them to remember

67

the power of the Lord God and the powerlessness of the Babylonian idols. The prophet reminded the people of the fact that the Babylonians had to carry their false gods, Bel and Nebo, from place to place, while the Israelites had a God who carried them.

Not only is God great enough to work in spite of our feelings and circumstances, but He also works *in spite of our aging.* While some people may view the elderly as being a burden, time does not change God's opinion of us. Young and old are the same in God's eyes. He sees His children as precious and helpless lambs that need to be carried and cared for by the Good Shepherd. Every person, no matter what his age, is totally dependent on the Lord. Because of His eternal and unchangeable love, He is more than willing to carry us and to bear our burdens.

Even though our bodies deteriorate as we grow older, our souls are continually growing stronger. Second Corinthians 4:16 tells us, "Though our outward man perish, yet the inward man is renewed day by day." We can face old age and death with confidence, knowing that "our light affliction, which is but for a moment, worketh for us a far more exceeding and eternal weight of glory" (v. 17).

God is greater than our aging. The Lord cares for us and is interested in our problems, no matter how old we are. I fear that thousands of elderly people are being forgotten and neglected today. But even if people turn against us because of our age, we know that our God never forsakes a single one of His "senior saints."

In Spite of Failures

When the Word of God is the foundation of your life, then that foundation is secure in spite of your feelings, in spite of your circumstances, in spite of your aging and even *in spite of your own failures.* The last verse of "How Firm a Foundation" contains some of the most encouraging words ever written:

> "The soul that on Jesus hath leaned for repose,
> I will not, I will not desert to its foes;
> That soul, tho all hell should endeavor to shake,
> I'll never—no, never—no, never forsake!"

The basis for this stanza is found in Hebrews 13:5: "Let your conversation [behavior] be without covetousness; and be content with such things as ye have: for he hath said, I will never leave thee, nor forsake thee." This verse in Hebrews is quoting another passage in which Moses tells Joshua to remain strong and unafraid, relying on God's promise to never leave or forsake him (see Deut. 31:6). This promise is as true today as it was then. Hebrews 13:5 makes it very clear that *God is faithful no matter what.* He always keeps His word. Even if all the hosts of hell should try to destroy you, His promise is "I will never leave thee, nor forsake thee."

We are living in an age when the winds of change are constantly blowing. Many people do not believe in an absolute standard of morality but base their actions on the feelings of the moment. People are judged on the basis of their possessions or position.

69

Society teaches us that our goal in life should be to satisfy our desires and needs. Because most people are building their lives on a very shaky foundation, when they experience failure or loss, they are unable to cope. Their foundation crumbles, and they fall into a deep pit of despair, depression and defeat.

The writer of Hebrews warned us against being caught up in this kind of materialism and behavior. Our lives should not be based on our feelings, our circumstances or even our experiences. When our foundation is firmly rooted in Jesus Christ and His Word, then failures will not defeat us. We can trust God to work in spite of our weaknesses and failings, changing them into victories.

The Word of God is the firmest foundation we can ever have. The Lord has told us that "heaven and earth shall pass away: but my words shall not pass away" (Mark 13:31). We can rely on every promise in the Bible, for God always keeps His word. He has promised to help us, protect us, carry us and be with us always. No matter what fears we may have, no matter how bad our circumstances may be, no matter how many times we fail, the Lord is greater than our feelings, our circumstances, our aging and our failures. He can, and will, work *through* us and *in spite of* us. Build your life on the solid Rock, and your foundation will be firm forever.

> "That soul, tho all hell should endeavor to shake,
> I'll never—no, never—no, never forsake."

I Am His and He Is Mine

Loved with everlasting love,
Led by grace that love to know—
Spirit, breathing from above,
Thou hast taught me it is so!
O this full and perfect peace,
O this transport all divine—
In a love which cannot cease,
I am His and He is mine.

Heav'n above is softer blue,
Earth around is sweeter green;
Something lives in ev'ry hue
Christless eyes have never seen!
Birds with gladder songs o'erflow,
Flow'rs with deeper beauties shine,
Since I know, as now I know,
I am His and He is mine.

Things that once were wild alarms
Cannot now disturb my rest;
Closed in everlasting arms,
Pillowed on the loving breast!
O to lie forever here,
Doubt and care and self resign,
While He whispers in my ear—
I am His and He is mine.

His forever, only His—
Who the Lord and me shall part?
Ah, with what a rest of bliss
Christ can fill the loving heart!
Heav'n and earth may fade and flee,
Firstborn light in gloom decline,
But while God and I shall be,
I am His and He is mine.

—Wade Robinson

Chapter 7

"I Am His and He Is Mine"

The image of marriage is used in the Bible to illustrate three different relationships. We first see this image in the relationship between Jehovah and the nation of Israel. He married the nation of Israel, as it were, when He entered into a covenant with the people at Mount Sinai. In the Book of Hosea, the Israelites are described by God as an unfaithful wife (see ch. 2). Time after time in the Old Testament, the Children of Israel turned to idols and false gods. The people broke their marriage relationship with Jehovah and unfortunately had to be disciplined for it. The Prophet Jeremiah lamented for the nation of Israel. They had broken God's heart because they had rejected their first love (see Jer. 2:2,5,31-33).

The Bible also uses marriage to illustrate the relationship between Christ and His Church. Ephesians 5:25 tells us, "Husbands, love your wives, even as Christ also loved the church, and gave himself for it." In II Corinthians 11:2 Paul warned the church at Corinth lest she become unfaithful to the One to whom she had been espoused. It is important for a local congregation to have a loving relationship with the Lord. In Revelation 2:4 Jesus said to the Church of Ephesus, "You have left your first love."

The relationship between Christ and His believers is pictured in many ways in the Bible. For example, Jesus is described as the Good Shepherd, while we are His sheep (see John 10:11-16). He is the Head of the Body (see Eph. 5:23; Col. 1:18); we are the members (see I Cor. 12:27). Christ is the Cornerstone; we are the living stones being built into the temple (see I Pet. 2:5,6). He is the Captain of the hosts of the Lord (see Josh. 5:14), and we are the soldiers (see II Tim. 2:3).

In addition to these images, marriage is also used to demonstrate the relationship between Christ and the individual believer: "Wherefore, my brethren, ye also are become dead to the law by the body of Christ; that ye should be married to another, even to him who is raised from the dead, that we should bring forth fruit unto God" (Rom. 7:4). What an appropriate illustration of the Christian life! In marriage, the woman leaves many parts of her old life behind. She leaves the protection and provision of her home and family to become a part of her husband's life. In return, she receives her husband's name, his wealth, his protection, his provision, his love and his home. Their hearts, minds and lives are meshed together into one. In the same way, the person who accepts Christ must leave his old life behind in order to become one with Him. When he does, the Lord not only gives the person His name but also His protection, blessings, love and an eternal home with Him in heaven.

No other book in the Bible illustrates this intimate union between the believer and the Lord Jesus Christ better than the Song of Solomon. While many people see this book as a story about a sensual love between a man and woman, it has much to say to us about the relationship that can exist between Christ, the beloved, and His bride. Three times in this book you find the bride saying, "My beloved is mine, and I am his" (2:16; see also 6:3; 7:10). In this short book, the word "beloved" is used 25 times by the bride in referring to her bridegroom.

It's interesting to note in the Gospels that the word "beloved" is often used to describe Christ. In most cases, this description of Jesus is used in association with God's love for us. When Jesus was baptized in the Jordan River by John, God spoke from heaven, saying, "This is my beloved Son" (Matt. 3:17; see also Mark 1:11; Luke 3:22).

The word "beloved" is also used a number of times in the New Testament to describe the Christian. In Romans 1:7 Paul called the Roman Christians "beloved of God." Ephesians 1:6,7 tells us why we are beloved of God: "He hath made us accepted in the beloved. In whom we have redemption through his blood, the forgiveness of sins, according to the riches of his grace." If you know Jesus Christ as your Saviour, then you are accepted in the Beloved. You can say, "I am His, and He is mine." Because of God's grace, you can enjoy the wonderful spiritual relationship that exists between Christ and the believer.

A Personal Relationship

In considering the intimate relationship that we can have with Christ, it is important to look at the characteristics of that relationship. Only when we understand and develop these characteristics in our lives can we then know the wonderful blessings that come from intimacy with our Lord.

First, the Bible teaches us that our relationship with Jesus Christ is a *personal* one. God loves each of us deeply and personally. He cares about our individual needs and hurts. He knows everything about us, even the number of hairs on our heads (see Matt. 10:30). While Christ offers His salvation to the whole world, He does so on a personal basis. Paul stated in Galatians 2:20, "[He] loved me, and gave himself for me." Because Jesus died for us individually, we must make a personal decision to accept Him in order to receive His gift of salvation.

Just as Christ knows each of us individually, our relationship to Him must also be a personal one. Do you spend time alone with Christ each day, or is your relationship with Him built solely around another person or institution? While radio and television ministries, the local church and other believers can all help us grow in our Christian life, we must not allow them to become a substitute for a personal walk with the Lord. We have only one God and one mediator between God and man—Jesus Christ (see I Tim. 2:5). This means that we should not allow any person, group or institution to come between us and the Lord. We have the privilege of coming to Christ and knowing Him intimately and personally. Let's not waste the opportunity!

An Obvious, Evident Relationship

When a person enjoys intimate fellowship with the Lord, his relationship to Him is not only personal but it is also *obvious and evident* to all.

In dating and marital relationships, you can tell when two people are deeply in love. They do not keep their feelings a secret. They continually talk about how wonderful their spouse or future mate is. When the two of them are together, others can see their love in the way they look at each other and in their movements. They do not have to work at making their love evident. They just respond naturally to the feelings within.

Likewise, the believer who truly knows and loves the Lord does not have to work at making his Christian life evident to others. In fact, he *shouldn't* have to work at it. His love for Christ should be obvious in what he says and does. Just as two people in love desire to talk about each other, our love for Christ should also compel us to tell others about Him.

In addition, when we have an intimate relationship with Christ, He will be uppermost in our minds. When two people are married, they do not plan separate lives. Before making any decision or plan, they take the desires and needs of their mate into mind. They live for the other person and seek to

77

please him. If they do not have a desire to please the other person, we begin to seriously doubt their love. Likewise, the Christian who is living for the Lord will seek His will in everything that he does. The believer's primary desire and goal in life will be to please his Beloved (see I Thess. 4:1).

When you love someone, you want to be with that person. You find it difficult to be separated from him for even short periods of time. After a time, you find that you not only want to be with that person but you have also become like him. It's interesting to note how much husbands and wives are alike. As the years pass, they grow to know each other as they know themselves. They know what their spouse is thinking and feeling. They develop the same interests and tastes. The mathematics of marriage are both interesting and beautiful. In marriage, one plus one equals one—two individual lives have become one.

This is the way it should be for the Christian. Our love for Christ should be so great that we feel pain when our sin separates us from Him. When we are communing daily with Him, gradually our lives will become more and more like His, until we finally achieve the Christian's ultimate goal—oneness with Christ.

A Deepening Relationship

In order to achieve intimacy with Christ, our relationship to Him must not only be personal, obvious and evident to others but it should also be a *deepening* one. Christians do not grow up, they grow *in*. While it is important that our faith be evident to others, the true test of Christian maturity is the attitudes, motives and desires in our hearts and minds. The person who is experiencing a deepening relationship with the Lord Jesus will not only have the right attitudes and desires but will be able to share these with Christ as he fellowships intimately with Him. Jesus Christ truly becomes his best friend.

We experience many surface relationships in life. Each day we meet people on the bus, train or street. Often we start a conversation with them as we wait. But once we part, we usually never see or think about them again. Many of us also have neighbors, fellow workers and other people whom we know casually. While we often see them and stop to chat about the weather or the football game, they never really become an important part of our lives.

On the other hand, most of us have several close friends, family members or a spouse that we know extremely well. It is with these people that we share our innermost feelings, needs and desires. We tell them of our plans and hopes for the future, and they often help us in making plans. They listen to us with their hearts as well as their ears and are always ready to help us when we need it.

It is sad to see so many people today who have no close friends or family members. They are usually lonely and depressed. People need and crave intimate and deep relationships. This is true in the Christian life as well. Unfortunately, many believers

79

only have a surface relationship with Jesus Christ and with other Christians. I have been in some churches where everything is so analytical, so cold, so logical, so proper, so formal and so dead. The people have no excitement, joy or fellowship. While it is difficult to tone down a fanatic, I'd rather calm down a fanatic than resurrect a corpse.

Have you shared your feelings lately with Jesus Christ? Do you feel really close to Him? If not, then perhaps you need to work at deepening your relationship with Him.

An Exclusive Relationship

The final, and most important, aspect of our spiritual union with Jesus Christ is that our relationship with Him must be *exclusive*. We can never develop a deep and lasting relationship with the Lord if we allow other people and earthly matters to come between us.

We can see the danger of courting the world in the lives of the Children of Israel. Throughout the Old Testament the Israelites were continually leaving God in order to worship the gods of the heathen nations around them. In the Book of Hosea, the Lord compared the people to an unfaithful wife. He told them that they had committed spiritual adultery. Because their relationship with God was not exclusive, their fellowship with Him was destroyed, and they were punished for their unfaithfulness.

We do not have to worship a statue or person in order to commit spiritual adultery. We are guilty of spiritual adultery whenever we place someone or something ahead of God in our lives. James 4:4 tells us, "Ye adulterers and adulteresses, know ye not that the friendship of the world is enmity with God? whosoever therefore will be a friend of the world is an enemy of God."

God designed both marriage and our relationship with Him to be exclusive. In marriage, when one partner is unfaithful, it tears the couple apart. Their relationship is never the same again. Likewise, in our Christian life we cannot have Jesus plus something else. In order for our union with Christ to be lasting and intimate, He must have exclusive rights to our hearts. The author of the song "I Am His and He Is Mine" understood the importance of exclusiveness when he wrote: "His forever, only His— / Who the Lord and me shall part?"

This does not mean that we cannot love someone else. Instead of causing us to become selfish and leave others out of our lives, loving Christ exclusively gives us even more love for others. In my own experience I have found that my love for my wife did not at all contradict or compete with my love for my children or for my mother and father. As you grow in love for a person, that love spills over and touches the lives of other people.

Why do we obey and serve the Lord Jesus? Because of His love for us. Jeremiah 31:3 tells us, "I have loved thee with an everlasting love." The Lord's great love for us causes us to be filled with love for Him. "We love him, because he first loved us" (I John 4:19). It's this exclusive relationship that

81

makes us want to be true to Him and true to Him alone.

It is hard to fathom just how deep the Lord's love for us is. We cannot understand why He would want to share His love with a sinful world. He loves us even when we do not love Him. Even more amazing is the fact that Jesus Christ did not just demonstate His love for us on the cross or declare in the Bible that He loved us. Instead, He shows us day by day how much He loves and cares for us. We can experience the love of Christ while lying in a hospital bed, while driving down the highway or while doing our work.

Where are you in your relationship with Jesus Christ? Can you honestly say, "I am His, and He is mine"? Just as we must work to make a marriage better, we must also work to develop a personal, deepening and lasting relationship with Jesus Christ. In order for us to obtain the intimacy and oneness with Christ that is every Christian's goal, our relationship to Him must be exclusive. When we are walking closely with Him, then our relationship will be evident to those around us. As we grow closer to Christ, then we will experience in a fresh, new way His love, joy and peace in our hearts.

Great Is Thy Faithfulness

Great is Thy faithfulness, O God my Father!
There is no shadow of turning with Thee;
Thou changest not, Thy compassions, they fail not:
As Thou hast been Thou forever wilt be.

Summer and winter, and springtime and harvest,
Sun, moon and stars in their courses above,
Join with all nature in manifold witness
To Thy great faithfulness, mercy and love.

Pardon for sin and a peace that endureth,
Thine own dear presence to cheer and to guide,
Strength for today and bright hope for tomorrow—
Blessings all mine, with ten thousand beside!

Chorus:
Great is Thy faithfulness! Great is Thy faithfulness!
Morning by morning new mercies I see;
All I have needed Thy hand hath provided—
Great is Thy faithfulness, Lord, unto me!

—Thomas O. Chisholm

Chapter 8

"Great Is Thy Faithfulness"

No other book in the Bible speaks more about sorrow and pain than the Book of Lamentations. The very name of the book indicates suffering and weeping. The Prophet Jeremiah wrote this book at a time when he was grieving for the Children of Israel and what had happened to them. The city of Jerusalem had just been destroyed, including the beautiful temple, and the people had been taken captive by the Babylonians. History tells us that this terrible event took place in 586 B.C. The people remained captive in Babylon for 70 years while Jerusalem continued to be attacked and plundered.

Throughout this book we can see Jeremiah's tremendous pain and sorrow at the unfaithfulness of Israel. In Lamentations 1:12, Jeremiah cries out, "Is it nothing to you, all ye that pass by? behold, and see if there be any sorrow like unto my sorrow." He continues in verse 16: "For these things I weep; mine eye, mine eye runneth down with water."

Why was Jeremiah weeping so uncontrollably? Because he realized that their plight could have been avoided if the people would have listened to the Lord's rebuke and would have repented. In the

Book of Jeremiah, the prophet had predicted their downfall and had exhorted the people to turn back to God. He gave the Lord's warnings time and time again, only to have the people persecute him for what he was saying. The people of Judah persisted in worshiping false gods and breaking God's Law. They refused to repent of their evil deeds. Consequently, the Lord was forced to mete out His judgment. They had brought the tragedy on themselves.

The heart of the Book of Lamentations is found in chapter 3: "It is of the Lord's mercies that we are not consumed, because his compassions fail not. They are new every morning: great is thy faithfulness. The Lord is my portion, saith my soul; therefore will I hope in him" (vv. 22-24). Despite the destruction, despair and death that surrounded him, Jeremiah realized that he still had hope because he worshiped a faithful and compassionate God.

God by His very nature is faithful. It is one of His absolute attributes. Even if the universe and man did not exist, God would still be faithful. The Lord also possesses relative attributes—how He relates to us and to the rest of His creation. Many times His absolute attributes are seen in His relation to us. For example, God *is* love (see I John 4:8). Even if the Lord had never created man, He would still be love. However, He reveals this love day by day in His mercy, grace and goodness toward us. Another absolute characteristic of God is His holiness. He did not have to create the universe to reveal His holiness. He is holy by nature. But His holiness is revealed to us through His justice and righteousness. God is also truth. His truth is seen in His faithfulness. Because God is true, He is faithful.

It is interesting that the Hebrew word translated "faithful" or "faithfulness" means to be firm, to be fixed, to be stable, to be steady. In other words, God is loyal and dependable. We can trust what He says and does, for He always keeps His promises. Deuteronomy 7:9 tells us, "Know therefore that the Lord thy God, he is God, the faithful God, which keepeth covenant and mercy with them that love him." In a day when so many people are untrustworthy and undependable, it is good to know that we have Someone who can always be trusted. In II Timothy 2:13 we are told that God remains faithful regardless of what we may do: "If we believe not, yet he abideth faithful: he cannot deny himself." God's faithfulness is not dependent on our faith in Him. The Lord's very nature means that He is steady, stable, fixed, dependable and loyal to His people.

Even though we are never sure of our own faithfulness or of the faithfulness of others, we still have hope because our God is faithful. Regardless of the difficult circumstances we face or of our failures, we can be sure of the Lord's faithfulness to us. Because He is loyal and dependable, we can trust Him to see us through every situation.

To Chasten When We Disobey

In what ways is God faithful to His people? In Lamentations we find the first way in which our God is faithful. He is faithful *to chasten when we disobey.*

Throughout the Old Testament, the Lord sent prophets to warn and rebuke the people for their disobedience. But each time the people persisted in their sin. Because the Lord is just as well as faithful, He was left with no alternative but to punish them. We read in Lamentations 2:17: "The Lord hath done that which he had devised [purposed]; he hath fulfilled his word that he had commanded in the days of old." God had warned the people again and again of the punishment they would receive if they did not repent. He gave them many opportunities to change, but they refused to do so. Since God is truth, He could not go back on His word.

Most of us have difficulty seeing God's faithfulness in His punishment and judgment because we do not fully understand the idea of chastening. What is chastening? It is God's loving discipline of His children. The Lord chastens us because *He loves us.* Hebrews 12:6 tells us, "Whom the Lord loveth he chasteneth." Thus, we should "despise not thou the chastening of the Lord, nor faint when thou art rebuked of him" (v. 5).

Few parents would deny the importance of discipline in raising children. We have all seen the results when a child is not disciplined. He becomes spoiled and unmanageable. When a child disobeys, the parent punishes him because he loves him and wants to see him develop good habits. If a parent doesn't exercise discipline, the child begins to wonder if his parents love and care about him. Every child needs and desires to have guidelines to follow.

The same is true for Christians. The Lord realized that we needed guidelines, so He gave us His Word to follow. When we disobey those commands, God knows that He needs to punish us in order to bring us back into line with His will for us. The Lord chastens those whom He loves so He can build character into our lives. While we don't enjoy punishment, we need to remember the rewards that come from it (see vv. 10,11). Then we will be able to say with the psalmist, "I know, O Lord, that thy judgments are right, and that thou in faithfulness hast afflicted me" (Ps. 119:75).

Because the Lord is faithful, we can be sure that He *will* punish us when we disobey. He always keeps His word. God loves us too much to allow us to continue in sin. Lamentations 3:40-43 states, "Let us search and try our ways, and turn again to the Lord. Let us lift up our heart with our hands unto God in the heavens. We have transgressed and have rebelled: thou hast not pardoned. Thou hast covered with anger, and persecuted us: thou hast slain, thou hast not pitied." Why was God acting this way toward the Children of Israel? Because they were acting that way toward Him. God will respond to you in the way you respond to His Word. God is faithful to chasten.

But with the Lord's promise to chasten us, we also have the assurance that His chastening will not consume us: "It is of the Lord's mercies that we are not consumed, because his compassions fail not. They are new every morning: great is thy faithfulness" (vv. 22,23). God never runs out of compassion. Even while He is chastening us, He is compassionate and merciful. His greatest desire is that we will repent so punishment is not necessary. He does not like to discipline us. He only does so in order to teach us (see vv. 32-35).

This doesn't mean that every time of trial and suffering in our lives is caused by sin. But this is often the case. I'm glad my Father loves me too much to let me have my way. Imagine the problems we could cause for ourselves if we always had our way. When God disciplines us, He does it for our own good. Thus, we can be thankful for His faithfulness in chastening.

To Confirm When We Are Unsteady

A second way in which God reveals His faithfulness to us is by *confirming us when we are unsteady*. In I Corinthians 1:7-9 we read: "So that ye come behind in no gift; waiting for the coming of our Lord Jesus Christ: who shall also confirm you unto the end, that ye may be blameless in the day of our Lord Jesus Christ. God is faithful, by whom ye were called unto the fellowship of his Son Jesus Christ our Lord."

God is faithful to confirm us to the end. What does this mean? It means that we belong to Him, and He belongs to us. Those who have accepted Christ have become the children of God. That standing will not change. First Thessalonians 5:23,24 adds, "And the very God of peace sanctify you wholly; and I pray God your whole spirit and soul and body be preserved blameless unto the coming of our Lord Jesus Christ. Faithful is he that calleth you, who also will do it." Because God is faithful, we can be assured that the work He has started in us will be continued until it is finished. Thus, since we have been cleansed and sanctified by His blood, we know that He will keep us pure until He comes again. Second Thessalonians 3:3 promises us, "But the Lord is faithful, who shall stablish you, and keep you from evil."

Why does the Lord need to confirm us? Because we are not as faithful as we should be. We often disobey His Word and do not depend on His faithfulness. One of Satan's most effective tools in undermining us as believers is to cause us to think we are self-sufficient. Most Christians reach a point in their walk when they feel they know enough about the Bible and the Christian life to go it on their own. They gradually begin to depend less on the Lord and more on themselves. The only time they really seek the Lord's guidance is during an emergency or a crisis in their lives. But the more they depend on themselves, the more susceptible they are to temptation and sin.

We can see the disastrous results of this kind of attitude. Marriages are breaking up, and churches are splitting. Christians are falling into many worldly sins and attitudes. We need to depend on the Lord and His faithfulness every day if we are to remain firm in a wavering world.

God is faithful. He will plant your feet on solid ground so you can stand firm and steady. When you are facing life's storms and temptations, He will establish you so that you are not blown about by every wind of doctrine (see Eph. 4:14). God is faithful to confirm you when you place your trust in His great faithfulness and power. What He has promised, He will perform (see Rom. 4:21).

To Care When We Hurt

God is faithful. Because the Lord never changes, we can trust Him to always keep His word. He is faithful to chasten us when we disobey and to confirm us when we start to waver. Our loving God is also faithful *to care when we hurt*.

Hebrews 2:17,18 gives us a picture of the Lord's great care and concern for us: "Wherefore in all things it behoved him to be made like unto his brethren, that he might be a merciful and faithful high priest in things pertaining to God, to make reconciliation for the sins of the people. For in that he himself hath suffered being tempted, he is able to succour them that are tempted." We worship a merciful and faithful High Priest. We can feel free to come to the throne of grace where He reigns supremely. At that throne we can find grace to help in time of need (see 4:16).

Because Jesus Christ is a *merciful* High Priest, He doesn't mete out punishment according to our sins. Psalm 103:10 tells us, "He hath not dealt with us after our sins; nor rewarded us according to our iniquities." God in His grace gives us what we don't deserve, and God in His mercy does not give us what we do deserve. If the Lord dealt with us according to what we deserve, who could stand

91

against His righteousness? It is only the grace and mercy of God that enables us to avoid eternal condemnation.

Christ came to earth as a man in order to make reconcilation for our sins. When our Lord died on the cross, He finished His work of redemption. While His work of redemption was completed in His death and resurrection, His work of sanctification is still unfinished. He is seated on the throne of grace as our High Priest and Advocate. He gives us mercy and grace to keep us from sinning, but if we do sin, then He pleads our case before the throne of God (see I John 2:1). Because the Lord is faithful, He will forgive and restore us when we come to Him in repentance.

When our Lord was here on earth, He went through every possible kind of temptation in order to prepare Himself to minister to us from heaven. Thus, He knows our situation and what we face. He understands and sympathizes with our every need. We have no problem that the Lord has not faced, no burden that He has not borne and no battle that He has not already fought. No temptation or trial is strange or unknown to the Lord Jesus. He was tempted in all points as we are yet never sinned (see Heb. 4:15). Jesus knows how it feels to be lonely, rejected, misunderstood and criticized. He has experienced pain, sorrow and bereavement. The Lord Jesus Christ enters into our situation today. He is faithful to care.

Because the Lord is faithful to care, we can trust Him with all of our needs. "Jesus knows all about our struggles, / He will guide till the day is done; / There's not a friend like the lowly Jesus— / No, not one! no, not one!" Thus, we can "hold fast the profession of our faith without wavering; (for he is faithful that promised)" (10:23).

This is also true as we go through persecution and suffering. The more we live for the Lord Jesus, the more we suffer for Him. Paul said to Timothy, "Yea, and all that will live godly in Christ Jesus shall suffer persecution" (II Tim. 3:12). Jesus also warned us of the trials to come. But with the persecution comes His promise: "In this world ye shall have tribulation: but be of good cheer; I have overcome the world" (John 16:33).

When we suffer because of our testimony and obedience to the Lord, He is faithful to care. First Peter 4:19 tells us, "Wherefore let them that suffer according to the will of God commit the keeping of their souls to him in well doing, as unto a faithful Creator." Even though we do not always understand God's purpose in our suffering, we need to commit our lives to Him and submit in humble obedience to our times of testing. The faithful Creator of the universe has everything under control. God is faithful to His creation; therefore, we can trust Him to be faithful to care for us when we are hurting.

To Control When We Are Tempted

A fourth way in which God reveals His great faithfulness to us is by helping *to control when we are tempted.* We read in I Corinthians 10:13:

"There hath no temptation taken you but such as is common to man: but God is faithful, who will not suffer [permit] you to be tempted above that ye are able; but will with the temptation also make a way to escape, that ye may be able to bear it."

Many people have the mistaken idea that once they become a Christian, they will no longer have a problem with temptation and sin. But they soon find out that they are plagued even more by temptation. We should not be surprised when temptation comes. We are still living with our imperfect human natures in an imperfect world. Our enemies—Satan and his followers—are fighting against us, trying to destroy our faith by tempting our fleshly desires.

While the Lord could shield us from these temptations, He does not work in this way. Instead, He permits these temptations, for He knows that the only way we can grow to spiritual maturity is by fighting some battles and facing some testings. We must learn to overcome temptation if we are going to grow in our faith. We need to remember that *it is not a sin to be tempted, but it is a sin to yield to temptation.* Our Lord was tempted, and yet He never sinned. Martin Luther once said, "I cannot stop the birds from flying around my head, but I can keep them from making a nest in my hair." While we can't stop temptations from coming, we can keep ourselves from yielding to them.

When we are being tempted, we need to remember that other people—including Jesus Christ— have suffered the same temptations and have not given in to them. God is faithful to control when we are tempted. What does He control? He controls the point in time when the temptation comes. He knows when we are strong enough to handle a certain temptation. He also controls the amount of temptations we face, for He knows how much testing we can take before we will succumb to it. In addition, He controls the kinds of temptations we face. Even when God allows Satan to use our greatest weakness to tempt us, the Lord will control the timing and the amount we are given so we can overcome it.

"God is faithful, who will not suffer you to be tempted above that ye are able" (I Cor. 10:13). Many people when they read this verse will say, "But I don't know how much I am able." But they are forgetting that it doesn't matter how much strength they possess, for *the Lord is able.* God is faithful. He will enable us to bear any temptation, either by giving us more strength or by providing a way of escape (see v. 13). However, we must be careful not to become proud of our ability to resist temptation. Along with this great promise in I Corinthians 10:13, Paul also issued a warning: "Let him that thinketh he standeth take heed lest he fall" (v. 12). When we become proud and overconfident, we are in danger of falling into sin. Peter confidently told the Lord that even if everyone else deserted Him, he never would. That same night, Peter denied Jesus three times (Matt. 26:33,34,69-75). It is only by the Lord's strength that we are able to overcome temptation.

When we are facing a temptation, we need to tell

ourselves, *God is in control. He knows that I can take this or He would not have permitted it.* Then we should expect God to provide the victory. He does this by enabling us to bear the temptation and by enabling us to escape it. These two go hand in hand. When we are being tempted, we must bear it until God opens that door of escape. The Greek translation of this passage tells us that He will with the temptation also make *the way to escape.* In other words, temptation is never a dead-end street. God always provides a way of escape. When Joseph was being pressured to commit adultery, he was given a way to escape it. He fled from the room (see Gen. 39:12). When Satan was tempting Jesus in the wilderness, the Lord escaped by quoting the Word of God (see Matt. 4:1-11). We always have a way out of temptation, if we will only wait until the Lord reveals the way of escape to us. God is faithful, and He is in control of our temptations.

To Cleanse When We Confess

Even though the Lord is in control of our temptations, many times we do not give Him control of our lives. Thus, we find ourselves yielding to these temptations. In our weakness the Lord's faithfulness is once again revealed. When we sin, He is faithful *to cleanse us when we confess.*

First John 1:8,9 reveals God's promise of cleansing when we confess: "If we say that we have no sin, we deceive ourselves, and the truth is not in us. If we confess our sins, he is faithful and just to forgive us our sins, and to cleanse us from all unrighteous-

96

ness." When we sin, we have only two alternatives for dealing with it. We can *cover it,* or we can *confess it.* Many people today try to hide their sins or deny (to themselves and others) that they even exist. While with their lips they claim to follow Jesus, their lives prove otherwise. They are only hurting themselves, for the Bible tells us, "He that covereth his sins shall not prosper: but whoso confesseth and forsaketh them shall have mercy" (Prov. 28:13).

How does God forgive us? He forgives us through the blood of the cross. The Lord is faithful and just to keep His promise. Because God knows His Son paid the full price on the cross, He will not punish us for sin that His Son died for. He will discipline us if we rebel against Him, but He will also forgive us when we confess our sins.

It is good to know that when we confess our sins, God removes the penalty of those sins from our lives through the blood of Jesus Christ. When we confess our sins to God, we tell Him exactly what we have done. "To confess" means "to say the same thing." Confession is not an alibi or an excuse; it's naming the sin we committed and admitting before God that it was wrong. If we want to receive the Lord's forgiveness and cleansing, we must be willing to take full responsibility for our actions.

Great is the faithfulness of our God. Unlike us, the Lord is completely dependable, trustworthy and loyal. He always keeps His promises. Because of His great love for us, the Lord is faithful to chasten us when we disobey, to confirm us when

97

our faith starts to waver, to care for us when we are hurting, to be in control when we are tempted and to cleanse us when we confess our sins. He understands and sympathizes with our sorrows and temptations because He has personally experienced every temptation and problem common to man. In each one He remained faithful; therefore, He can help us to remain faithful as well.

Hudson Taylor once said, "The secret of a victorious Christian life is not striving to have faith but looking off to the faithful One." We do not need to have great faith—only faith in a great God. When we place our complete trust in Him and become totally dependent on His faithfulness, then He will perform great things in us.

A Mighty Fortress Is Our God

A mighty fortress is our God,
A bulwark never failing;
Our helper He amid the flood
Of mortal ills prevailing.
For still our ancient foe
Doth seek to work us woe—
His craft and pow'r are great,
And, armed with cruel hate,
On earth is not his equal.

Did we in our own strength confide
Our striving would be losing,
Were not the right Man on our side,
The Man of God's own choosing.
Dost ask who that may be?
Christ Jesus, it is He—
Lord Sabaoth His name,
From age to age the same—
And He must win the battle.

And tho this world, with devils filled,
Should threaten to undo us,
We will not fear, for God hath willed
His truth to triumph thru us.
The prince of darkness grim—
We tremble not for him;
His rage we can endure,
For, lo! his doom is sure—
One little word shall fell him.

That word above all earthly pow'rs—
No thanks to them—abideth;
The Spirit and the gifts are ours
Thru Him who with us sideth.
Let goods and kindred go,
This mortal life also;
The body they may kill:
God's truth abideth still—
His kingdom is forever.

—Martin Luther

Chapter 9

"A Mighty Fortress Is Our God"

Most people recognize Psalm 46 as the basis for Martin Luther's marvelous song "A Mighty Fortress Is Our God." It was published in 1529 at a critical time in Martin Luther's life. The song became, as it were, the anthem for the Reformation.

Psalm 46 was also written during a critical time. During King Hezekiah's reign, around 700 B.C., Sennacherib and his Assyrian forces invaded Judah. They had surrounded Jerusalem and were planning to take the city. Sennacherib boldly defied God in front of the people, saying that He could not save them. But Sennacherib soon learned that God was in control. Hezekiah prayed to the Lord, and that same night He sent an angel, who killed 185,000 Assyrian soldiers (see II Kings 18,19; II Chron. 32; Isa. 36,37).

I believe that Psalm 46 was written shortly after this event as the people rejoiced in what the Lord had done for them. "God is our refuge and strength, a very present help in trouble" (v. 1). Did you know that the Hebrew language contains at least 30 words that describe various kinds of troubles? We can learn much about a nation and its people by studying their vocabulary. The next time you pick up the telephone directory, look through the yellow pages and notice the number of advertisements for automobiles, restaurants or televisions. How often do we talk about these items and others? They have become a big part of life in America. Vocabulary often reveals who people are and what they do. The Jewish people have suffered much through the centuries, and they have developed a large vocabulary to describe it.

This psalm assures us that in times of trouble and fear we can stand strong and victorious because of the strength and help found in our Lord. He is our refuge in times of fear. When we feel faint and weak, the Living Water sustains and strengthens us. We do not need to worry about the present or future because our God is in control. He is a mighty fortress. When our enemies are attacking us from every side, we can trust the Lord to protect us because He never fails.

Don't Fear—We Have a Refuge

When troubles come into our lives, *we need not fear because we have a refuge.* In Psalm 46:1-3 we read these assuring words: "God is our refuge and strength, a very present help in trouble. Therefore will not we fear, though the earth be removed, and though the mountains be carried into the midst of the sea; though the waters thereof roar and be troubled, though the mountains shake with the swelling thereof."

We live in an age of troubles. Earthquakes, volcanic eruptions, floods and other natural disasters have threatened the lives of millions. Many countries are torn by war and political unrest. Individuals also face many problems of their own, such as economic distress, illness and family strife. Many people fear the problems of the present and what the future may hold. However, even if we are facing the worst disaster imaginable, we do not need to fear because we have a refuge. God's strength is great enough to conquer any problem.

We learn several important truths from this passage. The first truth we discover here is that *we don't need to fear tight places.* Psalm 46:1 tells us that "God is our refuge and strength, a very present help in trouble." The Hebrew word translated "trouble" literally means "to be in a tight place." The psalmist was saying to us, "Don't fear your problems. Even if you are backed into a corner and escape seems impossible, you don't need to worry. God will make His presence felt. You can trust Him to help you."

The second truth we learn from this passage is that *we don't need to fear changes.* In verse 2 the Hebrew word for removed is literally translated "changed." Most people do not like change because they feel threatened by it. Changes cause us to lose our sense of security. But we do not need to be afraid of change, for even if everything on earth is altered, our God still remains the same.

Third, *we don't need to fear insecurity,* for "though the mountains be carried into the midst of the sea" (v. 2), God remains steady. This is quite a promise. Most people consider mountains to be

103

one of the strongest, most dependable and most lasting things on earth. But even if all the mountains were to sink into the ocean, we can still depend on the Lord. He is unchangeable and immovable. The reason that so many people feel insecure today is because they are placing their trust in other people, in money or in some other aspect of the world. But only God is completely dependable and trustworthy. Any other foundation will crumble under our feet.

When life seems to be collapsing around us and we desperately need to escape, it's good to know that we have a place of refuge. We can hide in the shelter of the Rock. But we need to remember that the Lord is not a refuge where we go to permanently escape our problems and avoid our responsibilities. God does not pamper us—He prepares us. His refuge is not a place of escape but of enablement. When we go to Him for refuge, He strengthens us and enables us to return and face those tight places, those changes and those insecurities.

The reason so many people fear life is because they are relying solely on their own strength. When we depend on our own strength, we are bound to fail. What is the secret of success? It is having the right Person on our side:

> Did we in our own strength confide
> Our striving would be losing,
> Were not the right Man on our side,
> The Man of God's own choosing.

Jesus Christ is our stable Rock in the midst of change. When life is collapsing around us, the Rock

104

is secure. The great Hebrew scholar, Franz Delizsch, has translated Psalm 46:1 in this way: "As a help in distresses, He is thoroughly proved." God is our refuge and strength. We do not need to fear the storms of life because the Lord has proved again and again that He will see us through them.

> And tho this world, with devils filled,
> Should threaten to undo us,
> We will not fear, for God hath willed
> His truth to triumph thru us.

Don't Faint—We Have a River

Many times problems and troubles begin to weigh us down until we no longer feel that we have the strength to cope. During these times *we need not faint because we have a river* to sustain us. Psalm 46:4-7 states, "There is a river, the streams whereof shall make glad the city of God, the holy place of the tabernacles of the most High. God is in the midst of her; she shall not be moved: God shall help her, and that right early [at the break of dawn]. The heathen raged, the kingdoms were moved: he uttered his voice, the earth melted. The Lord of hosts is with us; the God of Jacob is our refuge."

Throughout history rivers have played an important part in the location of major cities. When people began to settle in an area, they would locate near a river so they would have a ready source of water. Gradually, cities would spring up around the rivers. For instance, the city of Babylon was built on the Euphrates, Nineveh was located by the Tigris, the Egyptian cities were situated along the Nile, and

105

Rome was located on the Tiber. The people realized how important it was to have a river run through the city. If an enemy army encircled their city, they needed to have a source of water. Enemies knew that if they could cut off a city's food or water supply, it wouldn't be long before the people surrendered.

Jerusalem was one of very few cities that had no river. But King Hezekiah solved this problem by developing an elaborate water system, which you can still see in Jerusalem today (see II Kings 20:20; II Chron. 32:30). It began at the Spring of Gihon in Kidron and ran to the Pool of Siloam, about 1770 feet south of the temple area. When the people could not leave the city to obtain water, they did not have to worry because the system enabled the water to come to them.

Probably no other group of people understood the significance of a river better than the inhabitants of Judah. Thus, they were able to identify with the words of the psalmist when he wrote: "There is a river, the streams whereof shall make glad the city of God" (Ps. 46:4). What is this river the psalmist spoke of? It is God's spiritual supply of strength to His people. Jesus said, "If any man thirst, let him come unto me, and drink" (John 7:37). The Holy Spirit of God is compared to the refreshing water that strengthens and encourages us (see vv. 38,39). To the woman at the well, Christ offered water that would satisfy her so she would never thirst again— life in Him (4:14).

Water has often been a picture of God's provision. You will recall that rivers flowed through the Garden of Eden (see Gen. 2:10-14). When the Israelites were marching through the wilderness, God supplied water for them from a rock (see Ex. 17:1-7). But the ultimate picture is one Jesus gave us. When we drink of the water He gives, it will be like an artesian well of living water springing up in us unto everlasting life (see John 4:14). In other words, when we have placed our trust in Him, we will have everlasting life and can draw on His inexhaustible resources for our strength and sustenance.

Where is this river? Psalm 46:1 tells us, "There is a river, the streams whereof shall make glad the city of God, the holy place of the tabernacles of the most High." The river is found in the Holy Place. In order to drink at this river, we must have entered into the Holy of Holies through the blood of Jesus Christ (see Heb. 10:19-22). We cannot drink at that spiritual river if we are standing outside the city! When we drink of this spiritual water, we will not faint. Many Christians today feel like quitting because their endurance is gone. They do not have strength because they are not coming to the River daily.

Don't Fret—We Have a Revelation

Our God is a refuge in times of trouble and a river where we can be refreshed spiritually. Thus, we do not need to fear or to faint when facing the storms of life. In addition, we *do not need to fret because we have a revelation*. What is this revelation? Psalm 46:8-11 says, "Come, behold the works of the Lord,

107

what desolations he hath made in the earth. He maketh wars to cease unto the end of the earth; he breaketh the bow, and cutteth the spear in sunder; he burneth the chariot in the fire. Be still, and know that I am God: I will be exalted among the heathen [nations], I will be exalted in the earth. The Lord of hosts is with us; the God of Jacob is our refuge."

In this passage we find God revealing Himself to us. He told the people of Judah that He is the Lord of hosts (the Lord of the armies). Thus, they did not need to fear Sennacherib and his army because God would exalt Himself and would destroy the enemy. Instead of fretting about their situation, God told them, "Be still, and know that I am God" (v. 10). The secret to their victory was not in their fighting but in their waiting. They waited on the Lord and allowed Him to work in their behalf.

We are facing an even greater enemy today— Satan and his army. Satan is waging a war within us, seeking to destroy us (see James 4:1). When the pressures of life begin to close in around us, we often fret rather than trust God to take care of it. We become fretful about the Lord's timing and methods. God doesn't do what we thought He would, and so we begin to fret. We worry when it appears that our prayers are not being answered. Rather than waiting on God to handle it, we try to take care of the matter ourselves.

But the Lord says to us, "Be still, and know that I am God" (Ps. 46:10). The Hebrew word for "be still" means to keep your hands off, to relax, to let God be God. The Lord tells us that He will be exalted.

When we try to handle problems on our own, not only do we deny Him the glory, but we also create even bigger problems for ourselves. Let God work in His time and in His way so that He can exalt Himself in your life.

What could Hezekiah do about Sennacherib's army? Nothing! The only thing he could do was pray and trust God for the solution. And God gave the victory in a marvelous way. Many of the problems we face are similar. We can do nothing—although we often try and fail—so we should just take our hands off and allow God to accomplish His will in His way.

We do not need to fret because "the Lord of hosts is with us; the God of Jacob is our refuge" (v. 11). Notice that the psalmist didn't say that the God of Abraham is our refuge. Abraham was a great man of faith. We would expect God to help him. But Jacob was a failure, a schemer and a sinner. It encourages me to think of my God as the God of Jacob. We often act more like Jacob than like Abraham. But even when we fail God and try to do things on our own, the Lord promises that He will still be with us and help us.

Our God is a mighty fortress, "a bulwark never failing." He will help us ford the floods of life if we rely on His strength. We do not need to fear because He is our Refuge in times of trouble. He is our River where we can find spiritual strength and refreshment. God has revealed His great power to us; therefore, we do not need to fret when problems arise. Instead, we should rest in the Lord and wait

109

for Him to act in our behalf. When we do, then even the powers of hell will not be able to move us.

> And tho this world, with devils filled,
> Should threaten to undo us,
> We will not fear, for God hath willed
> His truth to triumph thru us.

Face to Face

Face to face with Christ, my Savior,
Face to face—what will it be?
When with rapture I behold Him,
Jesus Christ who died for me!

Only faintly now I see Him,
With the darkling veil between;
But a blessed day is coming,
When His glory shall be seen.

What rejoicing in His presence,
When are banished grief and pain,
When the crooked ways are straightened
And the dark things shall be plain.

Face to face—O blissful moment!
Face to face—to see and know;
Face to face with my Redeemer,
Jesus Christ who loves me so!

Chorus:
Face to face I shall behold Him,
Far beyond the starry sky;
Face to face, in all His glory,
I shall see Him by and by!

—Carrie E. Breck

Chapter 10

"Face to Face"

"Face to Face," a beautiful song written by Carrie E. Breck, is based on I Corinthians 13—the love chapter of the Bible. The focus of the song is found in verse 12: "For now we see through a glass, darkly; but then face to face: now I know in part; but then shall I know even as also I am known."

What will we know when we see Christ face to face? We will finally see Christ in all His glory and will discover the full extent of His love for us. First Corinthians 13 describes the kind of love that Christ has for us and that we, in turn, should have for others. If our Christian life is not based on the love of Christ, then anything we may do is worthless: "Though I speak with the tongues of men and of angels, and have not charity [love], I am become as sounding brass, or a tinkling cymbal. And though I have the gift of prophecy, and understand all mysteries, and all knowledge; and though I have all faith, so that I could remove mountains, and have not charity, I am nothing. And though I bestow all my goods to feed the poor, and though I give my body to be burned, and have not charity, it profiteth me nothing" (vv. 1-3).

112

We can preach powerfully and know the Bible well, but if our words aren't motivated by love, then we will not change people's hearts. We can perform great acts of kindness and sacrifice, but if we don't do them out of love, we will still not please God. Love is essential. What kind of love are we to have? Paul described this love for us in verses 4-7: "Love suffereth long, and is kind; love envieth not; love vaunteth not itself, is not puffed up, doth not behave itself unseemly, seeketh not her own, is not easily provoked, thinketh no evil; rejoiceth not in iniquity, but rejoiceth in the truth; beareth all things, believeth all things, hopeth all things, endureth all things."

Paul wrote these words in his letter to the church at Corinth. The Corinthian Christians were having problems in many areas of their lives—including their treatment of fellow believers. The church was carnal and worldly. The people were competing with each other, causing the church to be divided. They were using their many spiritual gifts as toys to play with and as weapons to fight with instead of as tools to build with. Each believer was using his gifts to try to prove that he was more spiritual than the others.

Notice that chapter 13 is situated between chapter 12, where Paul defined and discussed the spiritual gifts, and chapter 14, where he told them how to use these spiritual gifts. Spiritual gifts are worthless if they are not guided by love. The only way to serve God and to live with and for one another is through love.

Love is a mark of maturity. Paul wanted the

Corinthian Christians to become mature in their faith. Maturity isn't revealed in our spiritual gifts but in our love. We read in I Corinthians 13:8-13: "Love never faileth: but whether there be prophecies, they shall fail; whether there be tongues, they shall cease; whether there be knowledge, it shall vanish away. For we know in part, and we prophesy in part. But when that which is perfect is come, then that which is in part shall be done away. When I was a child, I spake as a child, I understood as a child, I thought as a child: but when I became a man, I put away childish things. For now we see through a glass [mirror], darkly; but then face to face: now I know in part; but then shall I know even as also I am known. And now abideth faith, hope, love, these three; but the greatest of these is love." As we obtain maturity in Christ through our love, then we will come to see and know the Lord Jesus better.

Seeing Christ by Faith

When Paul wrote about seeing Christ face to face, he was talking about when you and I stand in glory, when we are at home with the Lord. But did you realize that your Christian life began with seeing the face of Jesus Christ? Not literally but spiritually. Second Corinthians 4:3-6 says, "But if our gospel be hid, it is hid to them that are lost: in whom the god of this world hath blinded the minds of them which believe not, lest the light of the glorious gospel of Christ, who is the image of God, should shine unto them. For we preach not ourselves, but Christ Jesus the Lord; and ourselves your servants for

114

Jesus' sake. For God, who commanded the light to shine out of darkness, hath shined in our hearts, to give the light of the knowledge of the glory of God in the face of Jesus Christ."

We have not seen the face of Jesus Christ literally, but we can still have a personal relationship with Him. *We see Christ by faith.* "Faith cometh by hearing, and hearing by the word of God" (Rom. 10:17). When we look into the Word of God, we see Christ. He has revealed Himself to us in the Word so that we can have a personal relationship with Him. We can love Him even though we have not seen Him: "Whom having not seen, ye love" (I Pet. 1:8).

I will never forget the night when the light of God's Word shined in my heart. I had known about Jesus Christ all of my life. I had studied about Him in confirmation classes. I had heard about Him in Sunday school, church and youth meetings, but that particular night the light shined in my heart. I saw the face of Jesus Christ—not literally and not in a vision but spiritually. Having seen Him, I was saved.

I'm thankful that we can see the face of Christ by faith. In the Bible when someone turned his face away from a person, it meant he was rejecting him. If a king indicated that he did not wish to see a person's face anymore or if he turned his face away, it meant the person was dismissed. He was not to appear in the king's presence again unless he was called for. To be able to see the face of someone meant that you had his favor and blessing.

115

The Lord Jesus has not turned His face away from us. We are invited to come into His presence, and He extends to us His forgiveness, grace and love. But too often we turn our faces away from Him. We walk in the wrong direction—away from Him. Therefore, we have to repent, turn around and look upon the face of Jesus Christ.

Seeing Christ in the Word

Your Christian life began by seeing the face of Jesus Christ by faith. It continues as you *see the face of Jesus Christ in the Word.* Second Corinthians 3:18 says, "But we all, with open face beholding as in a glass [mirror] the glory of the Lord, are changed into the same image from glory to glory, even as by the Spirit of the Lord." The Apostle Paul compared the Word of God to a mirror here. He did the same thing in I Corinthians 13:12: "For now we see through a glass [mirror] darkly."

The Word of God is like a mirror. As we look into the Bible, we see ourselves as we really are. But we also see something else—the face of the Lord Jesus Christ. No matter where we turn in the Bible, we should be able to see Christ and learn something about Him. As we study the Word and become better acquainted with our Lord, we should grow and mature in the Christian life.

Second Corinthians 3:18 informs us of a miracle that can take place as we look into God's Word every day and see the face of Jesus Christ. We begin to be transformed. The word is "changed" or "transfigured." We become like what we focus on;

116

so the more we focus on Christ, the more we begin to see His character developed in our lives. We begin to reflect the glory that is part of Christ's nature.

Moses went up on the mountain and spent 40 days and nights with the Lord (see Ex. 34:28-35). When he came down, his face shone so brightly that the Children of Israel were afraid to come near him. Having been with the Lord, he reflected the glory of the Lord. He had to put a veil over his face to talk with the people. But eventually that glory faded away. What we need today are people who reflect the glory of Jesus Christ because they have been transformed by spending time in His presence. Then we would begin to make the kind of impact on our world that the early disciples did; they were accused of turning the world upside down (see Acts 17:6).

Seeing Christ Face to Face

When we were saved, we saw Christ by faith. As we continue in the Christian life, we see Christ in the Word. But a day is coming when you and I are going to see Christ face to face. The Christian life will reach its climax in heaven when we see the face of Jesus Christ literally. I have been studying my Bible for many, many years. I have read profound books of theology. I have studied the sermons of the great preachers of past generations. But I must confess to you that I still cannot comprehend what it will be like to see the Lord Jesus face to face.

Many people seem to talk about this future day so

117

flippantly and so carelessly. I think if you or I were ushered into the presence of the Queen of England or of the president of the United States, we would be overwhelmed because we would be standing in the presence of majesty and authority. But their majesty and authority is nothing compared to that of Jesus Christ! When we stand before Him, what will it be like?

Paul told us that now we "know in part, and we prophesy in part" (I Cor. 13:9). Today we are living and acting like immature children. "When I was a child," said Paul, "I spoke as a child, I understood as a child and I thought as a child; but when I became a man, I put away childish things" (see v. 11). He didn't just grow out of childhood little by little. Instead, one day he deliberately said, "No more of these childish ideas. I'm now a mature man." When you become mature, you have no desire to go back to what fascinated you as a child. Likewise, when you see Christ face to face, you will have no desire to go back to your old life.

"For now we see through a glass [mirror], darkly; but then face to face: now I know in part; but then shall I know even as also I am known" (v. 12). Paul was comparing the present and the future. He compared our present picture of Christ and His glory to what we might see in a faulty mirror. The reflection is distorted. The city of Corinth was famous for its mirrors, but they were not like our modern mirrors. They were made of metal—polished copper and tin—and did not give an accurate reflection. In the same way, when we look into God's

118

Word, we can see only a dim reflection of Christ's glory and the glory of heaven. This is not because the Word of God is imperfect but because we are immature. We cannot comprehend the glories of heaven because our minds are too finite.

The Apostle John wrote a couple of chapters in the Book of the Revelation that describe the glories of heaven (see 21,22). But it is as if he begins to run out of vocabulary. He has to use every symbol possible to describe what heaven is like. Even after you read what he wrote, you can't begin to comprehend it.

Our knowledge of Christ now is imperfect and incomplete. As Carrie Breck wrote: "Only faintly now I see Him, / With the darkling veil between; / But a blessed day is coming, / When His glory shall be seen." When we see Christ face to face, we will have an accurate reflection of His glory. Now we know in part; then we will know fully. This does not mean we will be omniscient. We are not going to have the same mind God has. I don't try to make this a test of anything, but I really believe that we are going to grow in our knowledge even after we are in heaven. One of the joys of being a Christian here on earth is learning more and more about the Lord. And I don't think that once we get to heaven we are instantly going to comprehend everything. I think we will continue to grow in our understanding of God's truth, God's Word and God's glory.

Today we view life as though it were an enigma. "Now we see through a glass, darkly" (I Cor. 13:12). The word "darkly" means an enigma; in fact, our

English word "enigma" comes from this Greek word. What is an enigma? It's a puzzle. We encounter so many things today that we cannot explain. People write to me: "I am going through this circumstance, and I don't understand it." I write back: "I don't understand it either, but I don't have to understand it. We don't live by explanations; we live by promises." One of those promises is found here in I Corinthians 13:12. One day all of these puzzles, or enigmas, will be solved. When we see the Lord Jesus face to face, we will understand many of the things we cannot understand now.

I really believe that when we see the Lord Jesus, we will be so overwhelmed at being in His presence that we won't even think of our questions. I have met Christians who were bitter against God. He did something in their lives that they couldn't understand, and they were bitter toward Him. They said, "I can't wait until I get to heaven. I want to talk to God about this." Well, when we see the Lord Jesus, I think we will be so amazed at His glory, His beauty and His wonder that we will forget our questions.

I have a feeling we will be like Job. Throughout the Book of Job we see Job saying, "I wish I could find God. I would like to take Him to court and put Him on the witness stand. I have a lot of questions I'd like to ask Him" (see 23:3-9; 31:35). Then God speaks to Job: "Job, here I am. What did you want to talk about?" (see 38—41). Job responds, "Lord, I don't have a thing to say. I've heard about You with my ears, but now I've seen You with my eyes, and I no longer have an argument" (see 42:5,6). When we

120

see Christ face to face, we won't even think about what seemed so important before. Our focus will be totally on Him.

I am encouraged to know that one day all problems will fade from view. As I carefully and diligently study the Bible, I discover many things I can't explain. As I try to help people with their problems and burdens, I find many things I don't understand. I'm looking forward to the day when I shall see Him face to face. On that day all the puzzles will be solved and all the problems will be explained.

Not only will we be able to see Christ face to face but we also have the promise that we will be like Him. In I John 3:2 we are told, "Beloved, now are we the sons of God [children of God], and it doth not yet appear what we shall be: but we know that, when he shall appear, we shall be like him; for we shall see him as he is." Revelation 22:4 adds, "And they shall see his face."

Unfortunately, on that day millions of unsaved people will be cast away from the face of God for eternity. They will never have the privilege of seeing His glory. Even worse than the fires of hell are the prospects of spending an eternity apart from the Lord.

But those who know Jesus as Saviour can look forward to the day when they will see Him face to face. Even if your body is racked by pain and your mind is perplexed, you can rejoice because one day those tear-filled eyes will feast on the glory of the Lord. On that day all your pain and suffering will be

121

forgotten as you rejoice in the presence of your loving Saviour:

> What rejoicing in His presence,
> When are banished grief and pain,
> When the crooked ways are straightened
> And the dark things shall be plain.
>
> Face to face—O blissful moment!
> Face to face—to see and know;
> Face to face with my Redeemer,
> Jesus Christ who loves me so!

In the Cross of Christ I Glory

In the cross of Christ I glory,
Tow'ring o'er the wrecks of time;
All the light of sacred story
Gathers round its head sublime.

When the woes of life o'ertake me,
Hopes deceive and fears annoy,
Never shall the cross forsake me:
Lo! it glows with peace and joy.

When the sun of bliss is beaming
Light and love upon my way,
From the cross the radiance streaming
Adds more luster to the day.

Bane and blessing, pain and pleasure,
By the cross are sanctified;
Peace is there that knows no measure,
Joys that thru all time abide.

—John Bowring

Chapter 11

"In the Cross of Christ I Glory"

Every person takes pride in some aspect of his life. Some people glory in their abilities—athletic, mechanical, artistic or musical. Others glory in their achievements. We often wish we could accomplish some great feat so we would be remembered and admired for years. We admire and envy those who are famous. When someone climbs a mountain, swims across a great expanse of water or explores unknown territories, we wish we could be like them. Many people glory in their possessions, but this is dangerous. Jesus said a man's life does not consist in the abundance of what he possesses (see Luke 12:15). Still others glory in their position. They are proud of the status they have achieved in their company or in society. In addition, almost everyone takes great pride in his family. Whether it is abilities, achievements, possessions, position, family or some other aspect of life, everyone glories in something. We can tell what is valuable to a person—what he would live or die for—by the things he takes great pride in.

The Apostle Paul had a list of accomplishments

that he could have been proud of. Before he became a Christian, he was one of the most well-known and learned Jewish leaders of his day. He stated in Philippians 3:4-6, "Though I might also have confidence in the flesh. If any other man thinketh that he hath whereof he might trust in the flesh, I more: circumcised the eighth day, of the stock of Israel, of the tribe of Benjamin, an Hebrew of the Hebrews; as touching the law, a Pharisee; concerning zeal, persecuting the church; touching the righteousness which is in the law, blameless." My, he had a lot to glory in before he was saved! But then he met the Lord Jesus Christ, and all of his values changed. What had been so important to him before became like garbage to be thrown away (see vv. 7,8). And what he had scoffed at and rejected before suddenly became very important to him.

After Paul met Christ he had a new list of things he gloried in: "Are they ministers of Christ? (I speak as a fool) I am more; in labours more abundant, in stripes above measure, in prisons more frequent, in deaths oft. Of the Jews five times received I forty stripes save one. Thrice was I beaten with rods, once was I stoned, thrice I suffered shipwreck, a night and a day I have been in the deep" (II Cor. 11:23-25). He went on to describe all the perils he had been through. Then he mentioned how often he had been weary, in pain, hungry, cold, naked and how, on top of all that, the burden of caring for the churches he had started weighed him down (see vv. 26-28). But Paul concluded that if he must glory in something, it would be his infirmities (see v. 30). He gloried in his sufferings because he knew they were for Jesus' sake.

The cross of Christ really touched the heart and mind of Paul. He never got beyond it. Paul is the great theologian of the cross. He has given us the deepest explanations of its meaning. This explains why he wrote in Galatians 6:14: "But God forbid that I should glory, save in the cross of our Lord Jesus Christ, by whom the world is crucified unto me, and I unto the world." Paul contrasted himself with the false teachers who were troubling the Galatian churches. Those teachers liked to show off. They enjoyed bragging about their religion. They liked to count their converts. They were trying to persuade all the Gentiles to put themselves under the Law of Moses. They wanted to glory in the flesh. But that kind of glory doesn't last. Paul said, "The only thing I glory in is the cross of our Lord Jesus Christ."

In our day the cross has become a piece of jewelry. It is something attractive that people identify with. But in Paul's day when you spoke of a cross, no one thought of a jeweler; they thought of a jailer. In that day the cross was something despicable. A polite person would not even mention the cross in public. It would be like our talking about the gallows or the gas chamber or the electric chair. Nailing someone to a cross was the worst form of execution in Paul's day.

But Paul gloried in the cross, and no doubt that was one of the secrets of the effectiveness of his life and ministry. What are you glorying in today? The test of a person's spiritual life is how he responds to the cross of Jesus Christ. I fear we have a crossless Christianity today. We have lost the true meaning of the cross. In America and many other parts of the world, it is so easy to become a Christian. You simply raise your hand or walk down an aisle. Nothing is wrong with doing this if it signifies a genuine commitment to Christ. But too often people want the blessings and benefits of Christianity without any dedication to Christ. Those of us who know little or nothing about persecution for Christ's sake have often made the cross something cheap. We haven't paid the price early believers did for their faith. In Paul's day if you identified yourself with the cross, you knew you should be prepared for rejection, suffering and even death!

Do You Know the Person of the Cross?

We need to examine the true meaning of the cross. We should ask ourselves three very important questions to discover our relationship to the cross of the Lord Jesus Christ. The first question is *Do I know the Person of the cross?* The cross itself would be meaningless apart from Jesus Christ. It was just a piece of wood; what Christ accomplished on the cross changed that wood into a symbol and gave it meaning for us. Thousands of people were crucified throughout the Roman Empire in ancient history, but their deaths were not significant to us. Only the death of Jesus Christ has affected the world. Christ, the carpenter, transformed the cross,

127

which was a symbol of suffering, death and defeat, into a symbol of glory and victory.

People make things important. Certain places and objects in this world are important because of the people identified with them. You can walk throughout the British Isles and find places and objects that have been preserved—not for their intrinsic value but because of the person associated with them. I once visited a door—a jail door! That door was significant because it had hung on the jail where John Bunyan had been a prisoner. Bunyan had made that door important. In the same way, Jesus made the cross important.

When you consider who Christ is, it should stir your heart. Paul said, "God forbid that I should glory, save in the cross of our Lord Jesus Christ" (Gal. 6:14). Let's examine Christ's name. First, He is the Lord. That means He is God. Back in Paul's day people would say, "Caesar is Lord," but the Christians would say, "Jesus is Lord." Several Roman rulers tried to make the people worship them and their authority—even to the point of claiming to be a deity. But only Christ has a rightful claim to the name "Lord." This name focuses on Christ's authority. Since He is God, this means God died on a cross for us. No human being could have died in our place.

Second, He is called "Jesus," which means "Saviour." The angel told Joseph before Christ's birth, "Thou shalt call his name Jesus: for he shall save his people from their sins" (Matt. 1:21). Jesus is the

Greek equivalent of the Hebrew name "Joshua," which means "Jehovah is salvation." This name focuses on Christ's humanity—that God became man in order to die for our sins.

Third, He is the Christ. This name is the Greek equivalent of the Hebrew word "Messiah," which means "anointed one." In the Old Testament, prophets, priests and kings were anointed, and Jesus Christ is our prophet, priest and king. He is our prophet because He is the Word of God— God's last word to mankind. He is our priest because He is interceding for us in heaven. He is also reigning on the throne, which makes Him our king. One day He will return to this earth and reign supremely.

In order for the Lord Jesus Christ to be our Saviour, He had to die. Peter did not understand that. When Christ first revealed to His disciples that He was going to die, Peter took Him aside and reprimanded him. "Pity Yourself, Lord," he said, "this shall not happen to You" (see Matt. 16:22). But it did happen to Him—deliberately, voluntarily and providentially. The death of Christ on the cross was not an accident; it was an appointment. The Father had appointed the Son to die on the cross, and the Son willingly gave His life.

I meet people who say, "Oh yes, Jesus was a lovely person. He was a fine teacher and religious leader." But when I ask them what they think about His crucifixion, they say, "Oh, don't talk to me about that." Some groups don't even want songs about the blood or the cross in their hymnal. Why? They have rejected the cross. Yet throughout the Word of God we see great emphasis on the *death* of Jesus Christ. The entire sacrificial system of Old Testament times pointed to the death of Christ. In Genesis 22:7 Isaac asked his father, Abraham, where the lamb for the sacrifice was. Abraham replied, "God will provide himself a lamb for a burnt-offering" (v. 8). Hundreds of years later, John the Baptist affirmed, "Behold the Lamb of God, which taketh away the sin of the world" (John 1:29).

You will notice that Galatians 6:14 doesn't say *the* Lord Jesus Christ; it says *our* Lord Jesus Christ. We need to make our relationship to Christ personal. Can you say, "He is my Lord Jesus Christ"? Can you say with Mary, "My soul doth magnify the Lord, and my spirit hath rejoiced in God my Saviour"? (Luke 1:46,47). Do you know the Person of the cross? If you do, you will glory in the cross.

Do You Understand the Purpose of the Cross?

The second question you need to ask yourself to discover your relationship to the cross is *Do I understand the purpose of the cross?* When Jesus died on the cross, He accomplished several things—both for sinners and for saints. You may ask, "Does the cross have any application to my life now that I am saved?" It certainly does. When Christ died, He accomplished certain things in society, in nature and in the universe. The reasons for the death of our Lord Jesus Christ are profound and wonderful.

130

For the Sinner

Let's consider first of all the purposes of the cross for the sinner. What is the meaning of the cross for the unbeliever? To begin with, it demonstrates God's love. Romans 5:8 says, "But God commendeth his love toward us, in that, while we were yet sinners, Christ died for us." And John 3:16 says, "For God so loved the world, that he gave his only begotten Son."

People often say, "When I look at this world and see earthquakes, volcanic eruptions, the spread of disease and assassinations, I don't believe that we have a loving God." Nowhere are we told that we can expect to see God's love demonstrated on the pages of *Time* magazine or in the local newspaper. Where do we find God's love demonstrated? At the cross.

When Jesus died on the cross, He fulfilled the Law of God. God does not break His own Law in order to deliver you from it. No, He is just. God's Law says, "The soul that sinneth it shall die" (Ezek. 18:20). Either you had to die for your sins or someone had to die in your place. The cross means that Jesus fulfilled God's Law by dying in our place. He has paid the debt completely for our sins. I fear we sometimes sing too glibly, "Jesus paid it all, / All to Him I owe; / Sin had left a crimson stain— / He washed it white as snow." The cross makes possible the life of God in your heart.

Let's examine three very important verses that tell us why Jesus died. "In this was manifested the love of God toward us, because that God sent his only begotten Son into the world, that we might live through him. Herein is love, not that we loved God, but that he loved us, and sent his Son to be the propitiation for our sins" (I John 4:9,10). Christ died so that we might live *through Him.* "And that he died for all, that they which live should not henceforth live unto themselves, but unto him which died for them, and rose again" (II Cor. 5:15). He died that we might live *for Him.* "Who died for us, that, whether we wake or sleep, we should live together with him" (I Thess. 5:10). He died that we might live *with Him.*

We glory in the cross because we know the Person of the cross. We glory in the cross because we understand its purpose in saving lost sinners. Christ died to demonstrate God's love to unbelievers. He also died that we might live through Him, for Him and with Him.

For the Saint

Many Christians do not understand the fact that the cross has a relationship to them after they are saved. We often think unbelievers are the only ones who need to learn about the cross. That is not true. The cross needs to be operating in our lives today. You and I must be living sacrifices. We must be able to say with Paul, "I am crucified with Christ [death]: nevertheless I live [resurrection]; yet not I, but Christ liveth in me [identification]" (Gal. 2:20). The Word of God teaches us that the cross of Jesus Christ is the secret of an abundant, victorious,

132

joyous Christian life. That sounds strange, doesn't it? It seems incongruous that something as ugly, painful and shameful as the cross could be the means of such blessing.

The Lord Jesus Christ was a carpenter before He started His public ministry. Perhaps the greatest work the Carpenter ever did was to transform the cross into a powerhouse for God. Before Christ was crucified, the cross had been an object of shame, weakness and defeat. Now it is a symbol of glory, power and victory. Jesus Christ so completely transformed the cross that you and I can live victorious lives to the glory of God.

This is one of the major themes in the Book of Galatians. Paul was dealing with the problem of legalism. The Galatian churches had been invaded by a group of legalists. We call them Judaizers. They said, "It's perfectly all right to trust Jesus as your Saviour, but you need Moses as your guide. Unless you keep the Law of Moses, you simply cannot be a spiritual Christian." We still have people like that today. They set up artificial standards for measuring the spirituality of others. They always want to add something to faith in Christ.

But Paul pointed out in Galatians that we have been delivered from the Law; we are now overcomers because the Holy Spirit within applies the work of the cross to our lives. For example, look at Galatians 1:4,5: "Who gave himself [Christ] for our sins, that he might deliver us from this present evil world [evil age], according to the will of God and our Father: to whom be glory for ever and ever.

Amen." Christ's death on the cross assures us of *deliverance from this present evil world, or evil age.*

John wrote to a group of Christians and said, "Love not the world" (I John 2:15). Paul wrote: "Be not conformed to this world" (Rom. 12:2). We are living in an evil world system. All around us is an anti-God, humanist atmosphere, which proclaims, "Glory to man in the highest. Man is getting better and better. He will become his own god." We are delivered from that system of thought through the cross.

The cross of Jesus Christ crucifies the world. Galatians 6:14 says, "By whom the world is crucified unto me, and I unto the world." It's interesting to note that the world has nothing good to say about God or Christ. Friendship with the world means enmity with God (see James 4:4). If we aren't careful, we will begin to think the way the world thinks. "Be not conformed to this world" (Rom. 12:2). Or as one translator has put it: "Don't let the world . . . squeeze you into its own mold" (Phillips).

Worldly Christians abound today. Why? Because they have never allowed themselves to be crucified with Christ. What did the world do to Jesus? It crucified Him. The religious world, the political world, the military world and the business world crucified Him. But on the cross Christ crucified the world. The world is dead as far as we believers are concerned.

The cross also delivers us from another of our enemies—the flesh. Look at Galatians 5:24: "And they that are Christ's have crucified the flesh with

134

the affections and lusts." Think about that. The flesh within us is pampered by the world around us. Wherever you look, you see something that pampers and entices the flesh. Pick up almost any magazine and turn the pages. The ads are trying to sell you something to pamper your flesh. So often they are decorated with nothing but sensual things to capture your attention.

The subject of crucifying the flesh takes us back to Romans 5 and 6. Romans 5 deals with Christ's death for lost sinners. Romans 6 talks about how Christ's death applies to believers. Romans 5 discusses substitution—He died for me; Romans 6 discusses identification—I died with Christ. Romans 5 tells us that Christ's death removed the guilt and penalty of sin; Romans 6 tells us that His death took care of the power of sin.

In Romans 5 Paul was talking about *imputed* righteousness—that which is put on our account. We call this justification. In Romans 6 he was talking about *imparted* righteousness—that which is part of our daily living. We call this sanctification. This is why Paul said in Romans 6:11, "Likewise reckon ye also yourselves to be dead indeed unto sin, but alive unto God through Jesus Christ our Lord." He was telling us how to have victory over the sinful flesh. You do it by realizing that when Jesus died, the old nature was crucified.

Did you ever stop to think that crucifixion is one form of death you cannot inflict on yourself? You can shoot yourself, drown yourself, hang yourself, stab yourself, poison yourself or gas yourself, but

you cannot crucify yourself. You can only *be* crucified. Therefore, how can you crucify the flesh? You
must surrender. "I beseech you therefore, brethren,
by the mercies of God, that ye present your bodies
a living sacrifice" (Rom. 12:1).

The old nature has been crucified with Christ, but
we also have been resurrected with Him to walk in
newness of life: "Like as Christ was raised up from
the dead by the glory of the Father, even so we also
should walk in newness of life" (6:4). It takes both
the crucifixion and the resurrection to assure victory in the Christian life. You need both Good
Friday and Easter Sunday.

Besides delivering us from the world and the
flesh, the cross also *delivers us from the Devil.*
Jesus said, "Now is the judgment of this world: now
shall the prince of this world be cast out. And I, if I be
lifted up from the earth, will draw all men unto me"
(John 12:31,32). This took place on the cross. Satan
is an absolutely defeated foe. At present, he is permitted to go to and fro on the earth because God
has some purposes yet to fulfill, but Satan is a
defeated foe. God has delivered us from the power
of darkness and translated us into the kingdom of
His dear Son (see Col. 1:13).

You and I cannot defeat Satan in our own power.
He is wiser and stronger than we are. He also has a
great many helpers in his demonic army, and they
are seeking to defeat us in our Christian lives. We
cannot defeat him, but we can overcome him
through the cross. "Resist the devil, and he will flee
from you" (James 4:4).

Do You Experience the Power of the Cross?

We have been delivered from the world, the flesh and the Devil by the cross. This leads us to our third question: *Do I experience the power of the cross?* You may say, "I thought the cross was a picture of weakness." That is only true from the physical point of view. Because Christ transformed the cross, the power of God is now available to us through it.

We need to understand that when we lose our lives for Christ's sake, we ultimately save them. When we surrender ourselves to God, His power is released in our lives. Then we can realize victory over sin and suffering. If you are suffering today, go to the cross. Jesus suffered there, so He knows how you feel and He knows how to comfort you. Only the cross of Christ can transform suffering into glory.

Perhaps you need to be motivated for Christian service. Are you serving the Lord simply because it is your job or because it gives you something to do? Are you serving Him because you feel guilty? Go to the cross. Nothing provides greater motivation than realizing what Christ has done on your behalf. His love for you will stimulate your love and service for Him. And when you grow weary, the resurrection power of the cross will provide the strength you need.

Once you know the Person of the cross and understand the purpose of the cross, you can experience the power of the cross. Christ delivered you from the world, the flesh and the Devil when He died on the cross. Now you must apply those benefits to your life in order to live victoriously.

"God forbid that I should glory, save in the cross of our Lord Jesus Christ, by whom the world is crucified unto me, and I unto the world" (Gal. 6:14).